37.95

D0965777

to hell and back

Meat Loaf

to hell and back
AN AUTOBIOGRAPHY
with David Dalton

ReganBooks
An Imprint of HarperCollinsPublishers

to hell and back

HarperCollins books may be purchased for educational,
business, or sales promotional use.
For information please write:
Special Markets Department
HarperCollins Publishers, Inc.
10 East 53rd Street, New York, NY 10022.

first edition

Designed by bau-da design lab, inc.

ISBN 0-06-039293-2

99 00 01 02 03 ❖/RRD 10 9 8 7 6 5 4 3 2 1

contents

PART 3   bat out of hell

PART 4 paradise lost

there are only two kinds of people in the world—
good people and evil people. no, wait...there's three kinds,
if you count crazy people, who could be either good or bad...or neither.
no, wait, wait, wait...

for wilma

PART 1

bat out of texas

bat out of texas

I wake up in a room I've never seen before. The blinds are drawn, the TV is on. Some talking head is delivering the news. The only problem is he's speaking French.

I stumble over to the window and peek through the blinds. Outside, I see a postcard lake. Men in plaid shirts are fishing in aluminum boats. Couples are water-skiing. I don't like the look of this.

Definitely a hotel room. You can tell from the alpine painting above the bed, and the drinking glass wrapped in crinkly paper. The

5

door to the bedroom opens into another room. On the table I can see a large basket of fruit wrapped in yellow plastic. Nice.

There is some stationery in the desk. "Harbor Castle—Toronto, Ontario." Uh oh. Last thing I knew, I was in Arlington, Virginia. How the hell did I end up here?

I call the front desk. What day is it? Thursday. Are you sure? They are. The show in Arlington had been on Monday, so I've lost three days. Not good.

There is nobody else here from the band or the crew. Maybe I've had another concussion (I've had more than my share). Or perhaps I've just slipped into another dimension.

Three days ago I was sitting with the band at a Holiday Inn in Arlington, Virginia, waiting for the *Midnight Special* to come on TV. Todd Rundgren was the host, and he'd gotten them to play the *Bat Out of Hell* video for the first time. No way would they put us on live—who knows what we might do? The show came on and everybody cheered and whistled. *Awright! Get down!*

What? They've edited out the guitar and drum intro. Instead, *Bat Out of Hell* starts with the piano riff going into the vocal. Calm down, Meat—you're not going to freak out *no matter what*, remember? We get to "I'm gonna hit the highway like a battering ram" and the tape slows down. Then it's all right again. Here we go, first chorus. *Damn*, they've edited out the guitar solo, too. But that's okay, I'm . . . staying . . . perfectly . . . calm. *Fuck* the guitar solo. At least the motorcycle bit is still in there.

Everybody is standing up now, singing along. We're heading toward the end of the song. But there's something very wrong with the tape. It starts *s-l-o-w-i-n-g d-ooooow-n* like I've taken some weird drug: "Never seen the sudden curve until *iiit'swaaaaaaytooooolaaa-yuut.*" I think maybe I've imagined it. Anyway, it's no big deal, right? You probably see this kind of thing all the time and just don't notice it. I start to relax and it happens again. And aagaaaaaaaiin. It's getting worse.

I close my eyes (as if that might help) and hear a voice saying something about "a revolutionary new advance in hair conditioning." I look up and see a woman tossing her long hair over her shoulder in slow motion. Is the whole damn *world* slowing down? I am completely disoriented. For a minute I think this might still *be* my video.

he said goodbye to innocence.
e said hello to paradise.
hey knew it would never be like this again.

Paradise by the Dashboard Light."
he spectacular new Meat Loaf single from the platinum
lbum containing the gold hit "Two Out of Three Ain't Bad."

MEAT LOAF. "Bat Out of Hell."
On Epic/Cleveland International Records and Tapes.
Songs by Jim Steinman.

Or maybe I'm dreaming. This is the sort of thing that happens in dreams, isn't it? "Doctor, I dreamed I was watching my video, but it was really a Clairol commercial."

No, this is real. Realer than real. They've simply cut off the end of the video. I'm sitting there, pathetically asking, "Do you think they will pick the song back up after the commercial?" They don't.

I'm throwing things around the room and bellowing like a big, wounded animal (big, wounded animals are dangerous). I'm also on the phone railing at "those responsible"—*whoever* they may be! Everyone I ever knew, apparently. Especially the people who worked for me.

"What are you doing? If this isn't your job, then whose job is it? I'm out here on the fucking road. I'm going to the radio stations every spare minute I have. I'm doing your stupid promotions. I'm doing the shows. Am I supposed to quality-check a videotape, fer Chrissakes, before it goes on the damn Midnight Special*? Do I have to take care of EVERYTHING MYSELF?"*

I remember leaving the room, getting on the elevator, and walking out the front door of the hotel. Outside, a sign said, "Keep *Off* the Grass." I didn't. I walked across the manicured lawn toward a bridge in the distance. Then nothing. Total blackout. I woke up in a hotel on some twighlight-zone lake in Toronto.

How had I gotten here? I don't mean the hotel and the lake and all that. I figured I could probably find my way home. But how had it all come to this? Dealing with problems by running into a dark tunnel and trying to disappear (or, even worse, trying to make *other* people disappear).

What was wrong with me? Didn't I have everything I'd ever wanted? *Bat Out of Hell* was number one around the world: a sold-out tour, limos, room service, dealers.

I lay back down on the bed and cradled the remote in my arms. The news guy was still speaking French, but he was my friend now—perhaps my only friend. There were pictures of dams and beavers and Indians getting out of canoes at some festival.

I got into one of those canoes. I was paddling down a long river. It went all the way to Texas. It ran by our house outside Dallas. My mom was there and my Aunt Mary was waving to me. I would be okay, now. I was home again.

the
vo-di-o-do girls

I'll start at the beginning. I was born on September 27, 1947, at Baylor Hospital in Dallas, Texas. My mother, Wilma, was a school-teacher. She taught English in the Dallas Public School system for twenty-five years. She was an incredibly smart woman—the valedic-torian of her class at Clarendon State. Her maiden name was Hukel. Wilma Artie Hukel. Where the Artie came from, I don't know—must have been some relative. Why else would you name a baby girl Artie?

My dad's name was Orvis Wesley Aday. Before I was born, he had been a policeman for the Dallas police force, and it was from there that he knew Jack Ruby and all those other people connected to the Kennedy assassination. We'll get to that later on.

Both sides of my family, the Adays and the Hukels, came into Texas from Tennessee. I've been told that Aday is a variant of O'Day and got spelled that way because that's how people pronounced it down there.

My grandmother's name was Charlsee Hukel, her maiden name was Norrod. She had four daughters: Texie, Cecil, Wilma, and Mary. Texie and Wilma, along with two other women, formed a little quartet, the Vo-di-o-do Girls. My mom had a powerful singing voice, something like Kate Smith's.

Among the many things I've lost over the years is a poster of my mother's gospel group—from when they opened for the Stamps Quartet in some little town in Texas. The ticket price was a nickel. I

was really impressed by that poster. To me, that was making it.

My mom and her sisters all wanted to go into show business, but being preacher's daughters, forget it—there was absolutely no way. The Vo-di-o-do Girls sang on the local radio station, KRLP, and from there they got on Bing Crosby's show. Bing Crosby had a syndicated radio program—it was taped and he would always close the show by saying, "And now for our gospel number!" The Vo-di-o-do girls would be in the studio and they'd do it live.

Texie went on to marry a guy named Frank Heath who owned a big chain of stores—Heath's Furniture Stores. They were huge in Texas in the fifties and early sixties. For Christmas, my parents would always get a couch from them or a new refrigerator. They had a big house in Amarillo. They were the rich relatives.

You know how as a kid everything seems bigger? Well, their house seemed gigantic. I remember driving to their place at Christmastime, being in the car, listening to the radio and trying to sing along. "It's a good thing you're never going to be a singer," my mother would say, "'cause you can't carry a tune in a bucket."

I stayed at my grandmother's house a lot. I don't know whether this was because my mother was busy teaching or because my father was an alcoholic and my mother wanted me out of the house when he was on a bender. My memories of childhood are all at my grandmother's house.

My very first memory is of the night my grandfather died. I remember my grandmother teaching me to play canasta. In the middle of the night I heard noises and got up to see what was wrong. My grandparents were both in the bathroom getting some medicine. There was a strange smell in the air that was somehow connected to his illness. That smell has followed me around the rest of my life.

That was also the night of my first concussion. After dinner I was goofing around on a footstool, jumping up and down on it, and fell off and hit my head on the corner of the table. Concussion number one—one out of seventeen, all told. I was big for my age, and clumsy.

All the Adays were big. And accident-prone. My dad's brothers were these *huge* guys. He had a brother named Elvin who worked for Affiliated Foods, and on a Friday night, they used to sit in the parking lot and drink beer. My dad was big, but Elvin was *real* big. So big that on one particular Friday night legend has it that he got drunk and got himself stuck in the trunk of a '57 Chevy. Had to be *cut out* by the fire department. That was just a typical Friday night around our house.

My father had a .22 shell in his leg from a hunting accident. He was real proud of that. He would walk around with his finger over the barrel of his gun to keep the .22 shell from coming out. Well, one time it misfired. Took the end of his finger off and lodged in his leg.

Early on my father raced motorcycles. He used to tell me a story about being in a dirt bike race that involved going through a creek bed. As he was coming down a steep ravine a calf happened to wander across the creek—he hit the calf and cut it right in half. Nice bedtime story, eh?

Dad was in World War II. He was a supply sergeant and one of the first to get wounded when the Americans went into Germany. He was in a boxcar when the first mortar shell hit, and got wounded in his leg. Not badly, but enough to be sent home. He never talked about the war.

The only time he ever said anything about it was one night when we were watching *The Big Picture*. We saw an airplane coming back to the States transporting the first American casualties from Europe. He just turned to me and said, "I was on that plane." That's all he ever said about it. After he got out of the Army, he came home and started drinking—and I spent most of my childhood looking for him.

trailerless trash

From when I was about four I can remember my mother putting me in the car to go searching for my dad, who'd be away for days. I would fall asleep in the backseat of the car while Mom drove around all night looking for him. We would wander all over Dallas, checking every single bar. By the time I got to be eight or nine I would tell my mom, "You stay in the car, I'm going inside." She would grab me and try to pull me back in the car, but even then I was too big to handle.

I think it was at those moments that my career as an actor began. I remember very clearly copping an attitude as I was about to go into the bar. Brave as I appeared to be, I was absolutely terrified. If I developed my acting skills anywhere, it was there.

Those bars were truly hair-raising. Hellholes. Back in the fifties and sixties there was a strip between Fort Worth and Dallas—and sections of it are still there, down by the Trinity River—that must have been the sleaziest, funkiest stretch of ground in the entire country. The most gutbucket, redneck, lowlife bars that you could possibly imagine.

I vividly remember going into those bars. The jukebox would be blaring; there were shuffleboard and pool games going on. These bars were filled with what folks used to call "trailer trash." A stupid expression, but you know what I mean. Actually, these people didn't even *have* trailers. It was *Deliverance* time.

I had to cop an attitude just to make it out alive. Being big helped. I'd look at these people and in my brain I would be saying, "Don't you come near me, 'cause if you so much as touch me, I'll kill you." Like that. Beaming out the vibe: "If you do *anything*, you're dead." And people would leave me alone.

Then my dad would come out; I remember *pulling* him out. He would never be mean or violent in there. He would come out and say, "Don't worry about me. I'll be right home." He'd never show up, though. This happened all the time. I got used to it. And I learned from it.

houdini and me

What I used to do, what I would *constantly* do, was run away. My mother would put me out in the backyard and I would just run. I would go down the street to the shops—my favorite place was the 7-Eleven. Any time that I was gone, I was probably down at the 7-Eleven sitting on the counter and talking to the guy who ran the place. He'd just keep me there because he knew my mom would eventually be down to get me.

I had to cross a big street to get there, though, and this was driving my mom stark raving mad. It got to the point where she would tie me up like a dog. Of course she couldn't put a leash around my neck, but she did tie me to the clothesline—with a rope around my waist.

Believe me, to this day I can untie knots better than anybody you've ever met in your entire life. I would sit out there and untie that knot, then go down to the 7-Eleven, where the guy would always give me a Dr Pepper and a hot Texas. That's probably why I wanted to go, I'm sure. The lure of the hot link.

But apparently once I got there and sat up on the counter, I would talk everybody's ear off. Just talk about anything, and I would eat the hot link and drink this Dr Pepper. And my mother would call up and come down there, and every single time she was scared to death.

Eventually my parents became so exasperated with my running off all the time that—I'm not kidding—they decided they'd better *move*. It was easier to move than to get me to change my ways.

Oh well, I figured there'd probably be hot links at the new place, too. Or other ways to get in trouble.

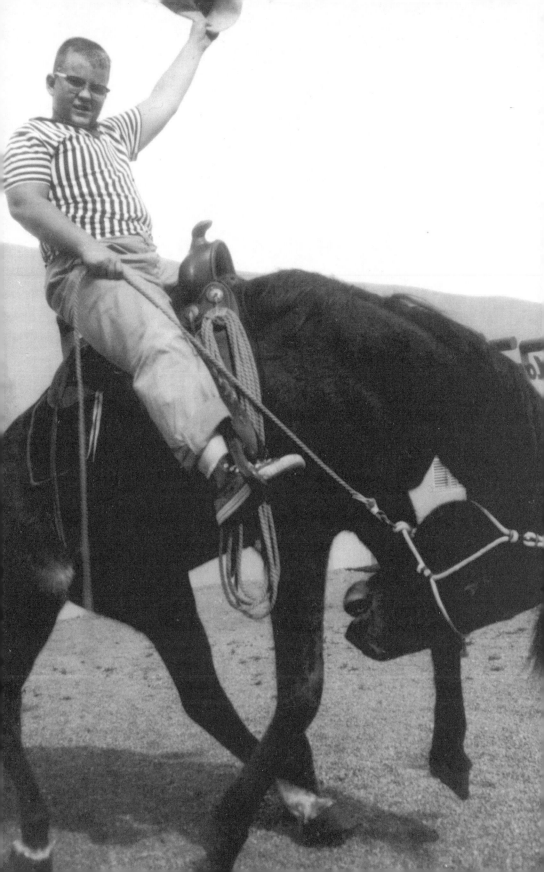

What you might call a little accident prone

So we moved over to this other little house, which was where I got my second concussion. I was climbing up on top of the swing set, and it had one of those metal glider things attached, like a seesaw. And somehow I fell off and sliced my head open.

It was also in that house on Kendall Drive that I fell into a wasps' nest. I was climbing an apple tree in the backyard with my imaginary friend, Bad Bob. When Bad Bob saw the wasps' nest he dared me to kick it.

"Nothing's going to happen," he said. "It's an abandoned nest. C'mon, ML, you're in the last nine yards, the crowd is going wild!"

I wasn't going to let the team down. I reached over and grabbed the ball—uh, the nest—and as soon as I began tugging at it I knew it wasn't abandoned. A horrible hum came from within. I tried to let go but it was too late. I fell right on top of it. You couldn't even count how many times I got stung. They wrapped me up in gauze and calamine lotion. I looked like the Invisible Man.

Tarantulas liked me, too. I remember one night we were having dinner in our tiny little dining room, and a tarantula jumped on me. Oh, they can fly. They can really leap, go from the floor up. It bit me on the only exposed piece of skin I had left: the tip of my nose.

There weren't any 7-Elevens near the new place—it was farther out of town—but there was something just as interesting: creeks. I always liked to play in the creeks, which led to the worst spanking I ever got. Once I got stuck in some quicksand and I came home barefoot and filthy. My parents were really mad at me. I remember being in the bathtub getting yelled at by both of them at once. Covered in mud in the bathtub, both of them standing there. Lost my shoes, lost my glasses, lost my books, lost everything. It all got sucked in. A harbinger of things to come.

Meat loaf, the christmas burglar

Around Christmas. The tree was set up in the living room, and under it was a present with my name on it. I really, really, really wanted to know what was in this package, so one day when my parents weren't home, I pretended someone broke into the house.

To make it look like a burglary I went through every drawer and emptied them all out. The silverware drawer in the kitchen, the clothes drawers, everything. My grandmother's room, my room, my parents' room. As if somebody would break into the house and open only that *one* box under the Christmas tree.

And you know what? I never got into any trouble. They never said a thing about it. I'm sure my father wanted to confront me with it, but my mother probably told him, "Now don't you say a thing about this! He's just a little kid and it's Christmas."

I remember going in the kitchen and saying to my mother, "I just came home and found it this way."

"Whoo!" she said, "what a mess. Can you help me pick everything up?"

"Sure Mom, I'll help you out." Nice guy, huh? I got what I wanted, by the way—a little rocket, with a white base and red fins.

The case of the Christmas burglar just got added to the family collection. Stories are like legal tender in Texas; the stranger the better. It's not that people in Texas are particularly morbid or anything. It's just that they love a good story, and the best stories naturally have some bizarre aspect to them.

My Uncle Carl's funeral was one of those.

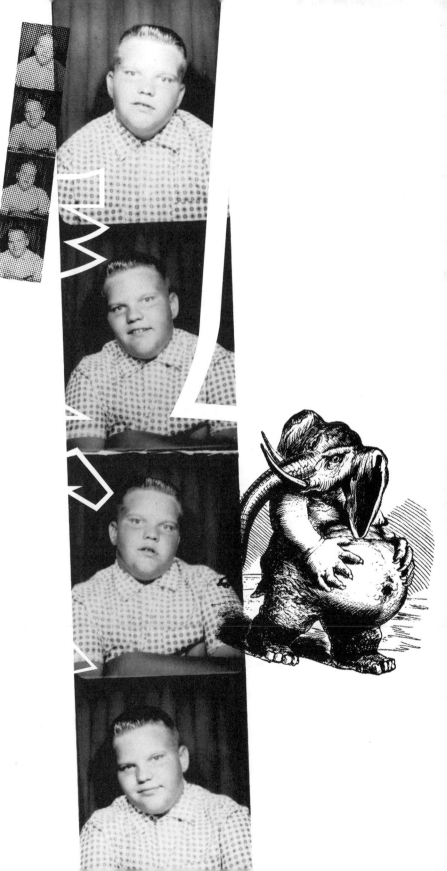

Death and texas

It was raining real bad the day of the funeral, and when that happens the tarantulas come up out of their holes. There are just thousands of them, and they get out onto the road. All the way to Uncle Carl's funeral I could hear this *pluk pluk pluk* as the wheels of the car squashed them.

In those days in Texas, they still used to hold funerals in people's homes. At my Uncle Carl's funeral, they had his corpse laid out right in the living room. The casket was up against the wall by the bay window, and directly across from the casket was a buffet. All these people standing around with paper plates piled with fried chicken and ham and mashed potatoes and gravy and, "How's your son doing in agricultural college" and, "Did you ever see a sight like that Molly Mae?" And a few feet away there's my uncle lying there in an open casket.

Well, I'm just about to tuck into my mashed potatoes and chicken when Grandma comes over and sits by me. "ML, you ever seen a real live walking ghost?" Now this was interesting stuff. "Can't say I have, Grandma. What about you?"

"Well, sure I have, honey. When your mama was a little girl in school, there was this set of twins just about her age. One day they were on their way home and a bad storm come up. They started running, but the lightning struck in the middle of a field and zapped 'em both.

"Can I get you some pie, ML? What was I saying? In the old

days there was a tradition, see, that when a child died someone had to stay with them in case they was afraid. People would come to the house and sit with the child until the day of the funeral. So me and this neighbor lady was settin' there in the parlor in the middle of the night keeping company to these two little girls when one of 'em sat bolt upright. My hair stood right up on end. The neighbor lady just took off down the road like she'd seen a ghost. Turned out only *one* of them was dead—the other one almost killed *me*." That's Texas surrealism for you, folks.

Those were the kind of stories that were handed down, and that's a lot of what children remember—the stories. Childhood memories are selective. I don't just mean what you remember, but *the way* you remember it. You never see the whole picture the way an adult would; you see the pieces you saw as a kid. It's like in *Peanuts* or *Ren and Stimpy*—all you see of the adults are their feet. That's my childhood. I see all the people, but without their heads.

For instance, when I was five I had my first picture taken by a photographer. I remember very clearly going and having that picture taken. But there are no faces. I can remember my mother holding my hand as we went upstairs to the photographer's studio, and the photographer's bow tie as he leaned down to adjust my jacket— but I can't see his face. I remember looking at that picture of myself for the first time and thinking, "So that's me, that's what I look like." I liked the way I looked.

the time we almost became millionaires

Did you know my dad invented Karo syrup? At least that's what *I* thought. My dad was a cop and then he was a salesman, a very good salesman. They used to say he could sell ice to an Eskimo. Once he sold a set of retread tires to a guy who didn't own a car. For a while, my dad, another guy, and my mom started their own company—the Griffen Grocery Company. Their only product was this corn syrup that one of them formulated.

At the Griffen Grocery Company my mom ran the office, taking care of books and things like that. My father was the sole salesman—he single-handedly went out and hawked the stuff. Went out to all the little bitty towns, 'cause they could never get the syrup into any of the big stores in Dallas.

They got a real thriving business going but because of his drinking my dad screwed it up. That company eventually became huge, but long before that he'd drunk himself out of the whole deal.

This was the story he told me, but subsequently my Aunt Mary laughed at the story and said, "Invented Karo syrup? Lordy, they been making pecan pies with Karo syrup since *I* was a child." So much for my delusions of grandeur.

Poor fat marvin can't wear levi's

I'll tell you the name I was given if you promise never, *never* to repeat it. It's no longer my "real name," anyway. I was so mortified by it that I had it legally changed. When I had my first name changed to Michael the judge asked me, "Now, Mister, uh, Meat Loaf, you're not changing your name because you are trying to escape some debt are you?"

"No, Your Honor. It's to shed something that's haunted me all my life."

"And what might that be, young man?" So I told him the story. Generally these legal things take weeks; he gave me his decision in thirty seconds.

When I was a kid I was really big. I was seven years old and I couldn't wear boys' blue jeans and I couldn't buy clothes in the boys' department. I had to shop in the men's department. And none of the Levi's they made at that time would fit me.

Then came this horrible Levi's commercial. The tag line was: "Poor fat Marvin can't wear Levi's." I'm telling you, I've never been the same since. After seventh grade, they put me on a diet and I lost some weight and I was able to wear blue jeans. But I was bound and determined that I would never wear Levi's. I *still* will not buy Levi's! I'll buy Wrangler. I'll buy Guess. I'll buy anything, but I refuse to this day to wear Levi's—I'm serious. Poor fat Marvin can't wear Levi's? What was *that* about? I remember crying over that commercial.

I didn't like the name, anyway. I hated it. From my first memory of when that name appeared in my life. And the Levi's commercial capped it. I would nevermore be Marvin.

People called me "ML" or "Meat." They never called me Meat Loaf that much. As I got older they called me Mighty Large, because of the initials. Or Mary Lou. My legs were so big that coaches would call me Tree Trunks.

"Tree Trunks, get over here!" My thighs at one time were

something like thirty-eight inches around. They had to put vents in the sides of my football pants 'cause they wouldn't fit with all the knee pads and all that. So they put these big elastic strips on each side of my pants, which kind of matched the others. But not really.

# How i got my name

My mother was an absolute angel. Whatever goodness I have in my heart comes from my mother. She adored me, which I think may have caused problems between her and my father. He was kind of immature in the sense that he wanted to be the focus of her adoration, and then I came along.

I never saw my mom lose her temper. She always said, "Two of us sisters had tempers, two of us didn't. But I'm not saying which." She was a shrewd psychologist. She'd always say, "If you really think you've got to do that. . ." and then she'd tell you what was going to happen should you choose to pursue that particular course of action. And it always happened just the way she said it.

Mom was very kind and also really smart. She brought me up not to be prejudiced. That's the one thing I remember her managing to drill into me. "There are good and bad people, and that's the *only* difference. Everyone—it doesn't matter where they come from or what they look like—is the same. Know that."

My mother wrote a textbook about communism that was extremely controversial at the time—this was the fifties, right in the middle of the House Committee on Un-American Activities hearings. She didn't go along with all the negative propaganda about communism; she just gave you the pure facts of what happened. It caused such a ruckus that they didn't use it at first, but eventually it was adopted as the standard text in the Dallas public school system.

My dad is the one who called me Meat Loaf. I've told a lot of other stories about how I got the name, about how football coaches and other kids called me that. How I made a bet with some kid in high school that I would let my head get run over by a Volkswagen and after I'd done it, this kid said. "Ya know, you're as dumb as a hunk of meat loaf." Or there's the one about the coach who said, "Get off my football team, you big hunk of meat loaf." All that actually did happen, but they didn't come up with the name. Leave it to my dad to do that. He called me Meat Loaf almost from the time my mother brought me home.

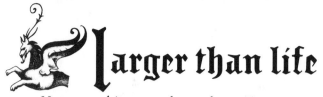
larger than life

Not everything you hear about Texas is true, and the same goes for me. But Texas is big and so was I. Even as a kid I was so big my mother started me straight off in the first grade instead of putting me in kindergarten—and I was *still* bigger than anyone in the class.

I was always adventurous, a rebel, and big and clumsy at the same time. I remember climbing up a very high wall to see what was on the other side, falling off, and cutting my knee and my head. Concussion number three. I still have the scar from it. And I still want to know what's on the other side of that wall.

I wasn't just big, I was *really* big—in the seventh grade I weighed 240 pounds. In the seventh grade.

I remember at this one school everybody teased me so bad, I think I fought every kid in my class. At the same time. Being that big, there weren't a whole lot of people who would fight you one-on-one.

Once I had a fight with ten or twelve of 'em at once. When they started coming after me I hopped into this ball box—they used to have these ball boxes in which you'd put all the balls after practice—and these kids closed the lid, locked it on me, and left me there. It was like *Bridge on the River Kwai.*

Nobody was around, either. The PE teacher had gone back into the school and everybody else was going home. They just locked me in it and left. There was *nobody.* I could just barely see out, 'cause you could raise the lid and see through the slit. I was screaming and screaming. It felt like I was in there for hours.

After we moved, I remember going down the street to play with this kid—I was in the sixth or seventh grade.

"Go away!" his mother yelled at me. "You can't play with my son, *you're too fat.*" Weird, huh?

There was a broom in the front yard. I got so mad that I picked it up and started banging on her window and . . . I broke her plate glass window.

Being too fat to play with the other children, I had to spend a lot of time alone, which probably has a lot to do with the way I am today. I'm usually alone in my hotel room from right after the show until the next day's sound check. And I'm never bored; I don't *get* bored. Probably because mothers wouldn't let their kids play with me.

four songs

I have no rhythm whatsoever, but I used to lip-synch to Tennessee Ernie Ford's "Sixteen Tons" while playing bongos. That was my favorite song! It's probably the only record that I ever bought until high school. I wasn't really into music like most kids; I just didn't get it.

"Sixteen Tons" was a proto-rock record. It had an R&B kinda beat, and the best thing about it was that anybody could sing it. Later on, it was Johnny Preston's "Running Bear." And "Teen Angel." Those were the three songs of my youth. I've never been obsessed by music the way some people are. To some, it's a religion. For me, there were three songs. There might be one more I could add: "Life in the Fast Lane" by the Eagles. That was it. Four songs.

I was different in the sense that I didn't have these life experiences that were connected to specific songs. The only music moment I have is that my car once got repossessed while I was listening to "Hey, Jude" on the radio. That's it. Later on I was really into Dylan and the Stones and the Kingston Trio. This was my record collection when I was a kid: Bob Dylan, the Rolling Stones, the Kingston Trio. I had all their records, and that's *all* I would listen to in my room.

Nothing else really moved me. Except Mahalia Jackson. My mother had all her albums and I loved her singing. My mother's favorite record was the soundtrack to *Oklahoma!* She listened to that all the time. I know every word. I still own a copy of it and I still listen to it.

When my mother had her bridge parties, she and her friends would always sing along with Mitch. Mitch Miller had all these sing-along albums. They were very into bridge in the fifties. Bridge and *Gunsmoke*, those were the big things. They'd have these bridge parties, and before the bridge game they'd all be singing along with Mitch. Like some bizarre suburban ritual.

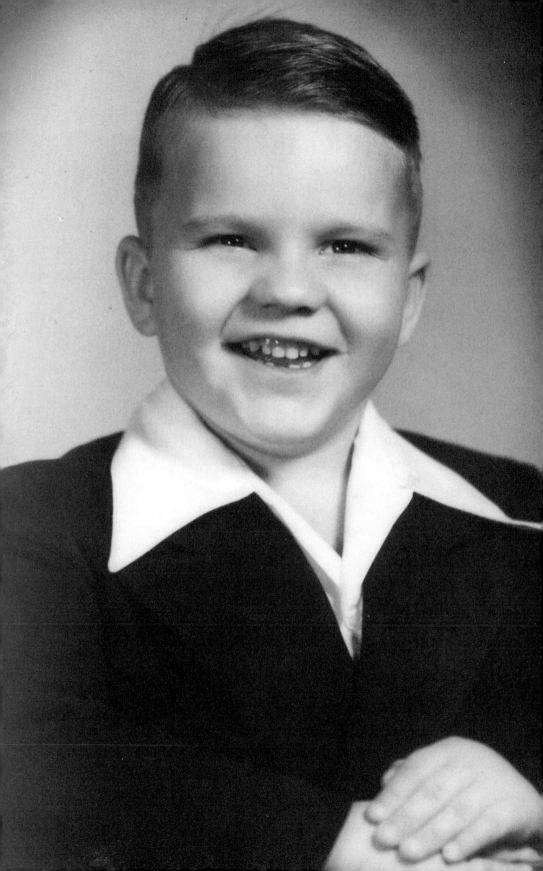

paper plates
and plastic knives

I only saw my mother panic twice. See the scar in the middle of my forehead? That was one of those times. You know how as a child you do things that are kinda stupid? Well, this was *very* stupid.

Me and this kid I used to play with both had these bows and arrows with little suction tips on the end. For some reason, this didn't seem all that authentic to us, so we took the suction cups off and put the wooden shaft of the arrow into the pencil sharpener. Made them nice and realistic. Then we started shooting arrows at each other, and one stuck right in my head. I walked into the kitchen with this stupid arrow sticking out of my forehead. I wasn't crying—I was more stunned than anything. But when my mom screamed, "Oh my God!" Then I started screaming and crying, and the arrow just fell out onto the floor.

My head was a magnet for trouble. When I was a little boy, I went through the back window of my parents' car. In the eighth grade, a kid whacked me on the head with his helmet as I was leaving the field and I went out like a light. In the ninth grade, I tripped over a bench and fell into an open locker in the middle of a fight with Randy Dyer (who administered the *coup de grace* by slamming my head with the locker door). Then there was the time someone kneed me in the head during a football game and I saw stars. Concussions number four through seven, folks. When I was a sophomore in high school I got hit in the head with a shot-put thrown sixty feet. Not an easy thing to do, but I managed it. I was a pretty good shot-putter—not as good as this other guy, but I was throwing fifty-two, fifty-four feet, which ain't bad. Even at the shot-put meets in the eighth grade I was finishing fourth in the city of Dallas. Of course, I *was* ten times bigger than anybody else.

I was getting better and better, and by my sophomore year, I was in the finals. We were warming up—one guy tossed while everyone else stood around at the perimeter, some sixty feet away. I'm idly chatting with this friend of mine when suddenly he turns white in the face, his mouth opens, and I hear him say, "MEAT, LOOK—" I didn't hear the next word. Never heard the "OUT!" I'm standing on the field at sixty-two feet and *bam!* in the head with a twelve-pound iron ball. Concussion number eight.

The next thing I remember, I'm on the ground and there are people running from everywhere. The sound of the shot-put hitting my head was so loud that the junior high baseball team playing three hundred yards away heard it. They said it sounded like someone had cracked a baseball bat. Coach Kirk, the defensive line coach for the football team, was there—he was the god of field events, and I remember him leaning over me and saying, "Meat, can you hear me? Are you okay?"

"Yeah, I'm great!"

"My God, are you sure? Can you move? Do you think you can get up?"

"Just give me a hand," I said, and started to get up. They're hanging on to me, propping me up, talking to me like someone who's come back from the dead.

"Do you know what happened? Do you remember who you are?"

"Of course I do, I'm fine. Stop holding on to me, I can stand on my own two feet."

They let me go and I tried to take a step. I moved my right foot and nothing happened. I tried to move the other foot. Left foot wouldn't move, either. Then I fell flat on my face.

Now people are going completely nuts. One problem is *how* to move me. I weigh around 280. They're trying to get me to the nurse's office. All these kids—there must've been fourteen or fifteen of them—dragging me like a wounded soldier off the battlefield, on this stupid high school wood and canvas stretcher. All the way across the practice field and through the gym. They get me into the nurse's office, and by this time the nurse had called my mother.

In comes Mom. She sees I'm delirious, but she's just relieved I'm alive—the same thing had just happened to a kid on the other side of Dallas; he'd gotten hit on the head with a shot-put and died.

They rush me into the ambulance, and it is flying. They're doing everything they can to get me to the hospital, driving over traffic islands, going up on the curb to get around traffic—it's rush hour. They're watching the traffic, but nobody's watching me. Every time the ambulance jolts I go crashing into these rails in the back. My head is going *clunk! clunk! clunk!* Bashing from side to side like a billiard ball. I can't speak and my head's so sore that even the sound of the siren is driving me out of my mind with pain.

All of a sudden I get really sick; I start throwing up blood. The attendants are alarmed; my mother turns pale. "Oh my God! Oh my God! There's blood coming out his mouth!"

This was only the second time I've ever seen my mother panic, and the first time I'd ever seen her *cry.* I don't remember *ever* having seen her cry. But now she was hysterical.

When she saw the blood she thought it was a brain hemorrhage. It wasn't. What happened was that when I tried to take that one step, I fell face forward, and on the ground was a little itty-bitty wooden stake marking the sixty-foot line. I fell on it and gave myself a bloody nose. The blood drained down my sinuses into my stomach, and I threw up. I had been okay in a dazed sort of way throughout the whole thing, but once again when I saw my mother go to pieces I panicked, too.

But in the end the only thing that happened—as far as I know!—was that I lost all coordination. I could barely walk or even speak. I certainly couldn't sing. I had been singing in the school choir but now that was absolutely out of the question. I was so sensitive to noise that even a ringing phone was unbearably painful. My parents had to remove the bells from the phone, we couldn't use silverware, we had to use paper plates and plastic knives and forks. People couldn't wear their shoes in the house.

Then, about six weeks later, I was playing baseball and Mitch Worley threw a curve ball and hit me right between the eyes. Concussion number nine. I was getting on real friendly terms with the folks down at the hospital.

Prodigal son

In the ninth grade, my junior high school football team played the Cotton Bowl and my dad came down. This is the only time I remember seeing him at one of the games. He arrived drunk out of his mind, got onto the field somehow, and started screaming at the coach.

"Why in hell isn't ML playing?" He was just so out of it, I couldn't explain to him I wasn't *meant* to be playing. The offensive team was in and I only played defense. But I was so upset by the whole thing, I couldn't play the rest of the game.

Whatever I tried to do, I was always out-of-synch with my dad. He was mechanical; I'm about the least mechanical person you'll ever meet. I remember once taking an aptitude test, and the guy who evaluated it told me I had an artistic, creative side. "You're not planning on doing anything *mechanical,* are you?"

"Well, uh . . ."

"Let me tell you something," he says. "*Don't.*" He didn't know how right he was.

Around that time, everybody was buying wooden steering wheels and putting them on their cars. I wanted one in the worst way, so I went over to Western Auto and bought one. Took it home and got set to install it on my '58 Buick. I got the horn off, and underneath it were all these, uh, *things.* I started unscrewing everything, but when I took the steering wheel off, all this stuff flew out! Springs and what have you.

And I'm going, "Oh no!" Because up to this point I'd been carefully watching how to put everything back. I had no idea where any of these other things went. Also, I now had to drive to football practice without a steering wheel—using a crescent wrench! Luckily it was just a straight shot up Walnut Avenue from our house. Couldn't have been more than a mile and a half up the road. Still.

love field

Kennedy was coming! This was a really big deal in Dallas, and so they allowed the kids to miss school—you just had to bring a note from your parents and then you were dismissed. I was fourteen at the time.

So Billy Slocum and another football player named Jimmy McCorder and I decided to drive out to Love Field to see Kennedy arrive. Jimmy's father worked there, and we figured he might be able to get us close to the president. We managed to be there when Kennedy's plane landed, but we couldn't even get *close* to the fences. People everywhere. Then Jimmy said, "You know, my dad thinks they're gonna bring him out of this side gate," so we said, "Okay, let's go!"

We drove over to this particular gate. There were a couple of Dallas policemen there and maybe another ten people. And lo and behold, that's the gate Kennedy came through. Right before he got to the gate we were standing around joking and Billy asked one of the cops, "What would you do if I had a gun?" and the cop just laughed and said, "I wouldn't do anything—long as I didn't *see* it." They were all laughing. And another cop said, "Well, yep, you know what? If somebody *was* going to shoot him, they would certainly do it here in Dallas."

As Kennedy came through the gate they actually stopped the car. I couldn't believe it. Billy went over with a couple of other people and shook his hand. I was very shy; I just stood and watched. And then he drove on through. Now we're all wired and we decide to go down to Market Hall, which was on the route. Since it was going to be a while before Kennedy got there we decided to go have lunch at a little barbecue place. Then we went to Mickey Mantle's bowling alley. We started to go down the stairs and saw they were blocked off—the place was being renovated. We went back up the stairs and saw a receptionist there. She had a little transistor radio, and as we went in the door she said, "The President's been shot!"

Jimmy put the little earplug from her transistor in his ear. "Jesus, she's right," he was shouting. "They're saying the President's been shot."

We went running off through the parking lot, screaming to everybody, "The President's been shot! The President's been shot!" and everybody's going, "You kids just *cut that out*."

We jumped in the car and headed for Parkland Hospital. That's where you went to watch the emergency cases come in when you were in high school. Typical Texas fun. You'd park outside and wait for the ambulances. Parkland is where they'd bring in gunshot victims and all kinds of horrible accidents. A ghoulish teenage form of entertainment.

Anyway, you eventually come down a long driveway and pull to your right toward the emergency room. But suddenly there's a guy in the middle of the street jumping from side to side, waving his arms for us to stop.

We pull over and the guy, I swear, takes out his badge. "Secret Service," he says. "Move over, I'm driving." I scoot over, and he drives the car to Parkland Hospital. We pull in, and there are guns everywhere.

The Secret Service guy gets out of the car and he tells us, "Whatever you do, DO NOT GET OUT OF THE CAR! Do you understand? Stay-in-the-car!" So we sat in that car and waited. We were there when the limousine carrying Kennedy pulled in. Saw Jackie get out of the car, saw them get Texas governor John Connally out. But we couldn't see Kennedy; we didn't see him at all. We sat in that car for the longest time and nobody said anything. Then a spokesman from the hospital came out and announced that Kennedy was dead.

We weren't allowed to leave. There were guys on the ground with guns everywhere preventing anyone from going out of the parking lot.

After another forty-five minutes we began to get antsy. There were so many people running around, we figured what difference would three more people make? Eventually we just said, "Ah, to hell with it, let's get out and see what's going on."

We started walking around and there were all these senators and officials milling around. You know that picture of all those black ladies sitting on the ground crying? We were right there.

Eventually the Secret Service guy came back over to us and offered to pay us for the gas. He pulled out a hundred-dollar-bill. And we said, "Oh no." And he said, "Well, at least let me give you five dollars." So we took the five dollars and we tore it into three pieces and each of us took a piece as a memento.

When we got back, nobody would believe us. Even though football practice was canceled, they were really mad at us because we weren't there when we were supposed to be. We tried to tell them, "Look, we were involved in this incredible adventure, we were at the hospital." Nobody took us seriously, but that night we saw ourselves on television, standing next to a senator from Illinois.

Subsequently, I read that there were no Secret Service agents in Dallas that day, other than those in cars. So who *was* that guy?

There are theorists who believe that a lot of people knew Kennedy was going to get shot. There are too many coincidences, too many strange things. You know, the odds of everybody who was involved dying within a certain amount of time after the assassination are just unbelievable. The taxi driver, the bus driver, Jack Ruby, Oswald, the stripper? The stripper who got gunned down outside Jack Ruby's club? What are the odds that all the people who were in some contact with Oswald would have died? From cancer? From heart attacks? The bus driver died of a heart attack on his bus. A taxi blowing up? How often does *that* happen?

And, as you probably know, the Warren Commission Report is the stupidest book ever written. I mean, it's just the dumbest thing ever foisted on the American public. Have you seen the picture of Lee Harvey Oswald standing on the steps of the Book Depository building just *watching* as Kennedy's car goes by?

Not that I know who did it. I don't. The mob? The Giancana people is one theory, because of what happened—how they helped get Kennedy elected and then he turned on them. There's even a theory that says Woody Harrelson's dad was involved in it! They say that Woody Harrelson's dad was the gunman at the fence by the railroad tracks.

It's kind of crazy that nobody, after all these years, knows. I went up to Bette Midler's house for a party for *Rocky Horror*, and there was some guy there who was supposed to have something to do with the Mexican mafia. Well, at some point in the evening I just turned to him and said, "Do you know who killed Kennedy?"

And he looked at me and said, "If I was you, I would never ask that question again. And I'd be careful where I did ask that question."

Now that gave me the shivers. Scared the hell out of me. I got up and walked out to the kitchen and stayed there until he left.

My dad knew Jack Ruby—and having been on the Dallas police force, he knew most of the cops down there. He always said that those policemen knew that Jack Ruby was going to shoot Oswald. That's the only way Ruby could have gotten in. And, because of all the little circumstances, my dad always thought the police knew that somebody was going to shoot Kennedy. None of those politicians down there liked Kennedy. And Kennedy had actually been warned when he was in Fort Worth. Everybody knew there were death threats when he came to Dallas.

My dad said it was just like the Pearl Harbor thing. There were plenty of warnings, but it happened anyway.

Early halloween

In Texas you had a lot of instant millionaires—oil, mainly—but it was just in the nature of the place. Hillbillies one minute, high society the next. I went to high school with a guy named Ricky Cobb; his dad had been Lamar Hunt's pilot. Lamar Hunt had his own Lear Jet, a very unusual thing in Texas, especially since HL, his father, was known for taking the bus to work every day and bringing along a brown-bag lunch.

I remember riding over in the back seat of a prototype of a Shelby Cobra Mustang with Indy race car driver Carroll Shelby, Billy Slocum, and Ricky Cobb. That was the first time I'd seen chicken fingers! Breast of chicken in strips, no bones or anything, and fried to

perfection! You gotta remember, this was pretty rich fare in Texas, where you grow up on white gravy with bacon broken up in it and you call it breakfast. A little cinnamon toast, grape juice, fried okra, black-eyed peas, and there's your menu. Given a diet like that, you aren't going to end up with a gourmet palate.

The Hunts' fortune was a couple of generations old—that's real gentry in Texas. The results are a little scary. The father of a guy I went to school with had been a maintenance man at Neiman Marcus in downtown Dallas. It caught on fire, and during the reconstruction he came up with the idea for the sprinklers. So this guy went from having almost nothing to being incredibly wealthy—him and his son had four or five Corvettes. Three people in the house, seven cars in the garage.

The interior decoration left a lot to be desired. People would walk into the house and go, "Oh my God! I can't believe my eyes!"

"Why, thank you," they'd say. Took it as a compliment. I'll just describe the master bedroom for you. The son showed it off to me and it was just about the most horrifying sight I'd ever seen. The entire room was black and orange. To this day, when I picture the black bed and mirrors with orange curtains I cringe. It was decorated in "early Halloween."

She was wearing no underwear

The first play that I ever did was *The Bad Seed* in high school. I played Colonel Penmark. We did it in the round—it was a boxing-ring type deal. All the characters stood on the stage the entire time. Never left the stage. Colonel Penmark was in only the very opening scene and the very last scene, so I had to stand there on stage looking straight ahead for the whole play. I stood there and stood there and stood there. Then I had some lines in the last scene again.

I was also in a lot of musicals in high school. *Charley's Aunt* was the first one I did. I played the butler and I had three lines. Then I was in *The Music Man.* I was a salesman on the train. Again I had maybe three lines. I loved it, though.

In my senior year they announced auditions for *Plain and Fancy.* Billy and I and some friends were out drinking beer, and someone said, "I dare you to go in and audition for that." I wasn't real drunk, but I was pretty lit.

"You're on," I said.

I went in as a joke and sang I don't remember what. I had everybody laughing. When they announced the leads of the musical the next day over the loud speaker they said that M. L. Aday got the role of Ezra.

What? I had gone in on a lark and landed a big part. I had two whole songs. That was when Coach Hayes told me, "You've got to choose between baseball and that sissy acting stuff because I'll tell you this: You can't do both."

"Well, that's fine with me," I said, "because I am doing the musical." I've always been this big ham, obviously, and here was my cue to really go to town. In one scene I was supposed to go into the leading lady's bedroom drunk and start taking off my clothes. I decided to improvise. People had been laughing at my other performances, so I thought, "Now's my chance to do something really funny."

I put on eight pairs of socks, three shirts, and two pairs of pants. And as I started taking off one *more* pair of socks, another shirt, and a second pair of pants, people were in hysterics. Huge applause. I got a write-up in the *Dallas Morning News.*

And as a result of that I got invited to do a walk-on in *Carmen,* in the chorus. They wanted me to be a soldier—carry a spear, and wear one of those helmets and say, "Aaaahhhh! Aaaaahhh! Aaahh!"

It was my first encounter with dyed-in-the-wool bohemians. I went down to the audition but I got so freaked out at these opera people that in the end I didn't do it. I'm sitting there, and I'm fairly naive, believe me, and I'm going, "What in the *world*?"

"Just watch the rehearsal," they said. "We'll call you when it's time for you to march on." They were going to dress us as soldiers and we were going to march on, singing. The girl who was playing the lead came downstage, sat down on a chair, and spread her legs for all the high school boys—and she was wearing no underwear! She just lifted her skirt while she was talking, and believe me she knew exactly what she was doing. She was having fun with us.

That night they had a party, and it was one of the wildest things I have ever witnessed in my entire life. There were people fucking in the bushes, on the lawn, everywhere. They were all running around half-naked in the backyard like one of those soft-core B movies. Totally freaked me out. It was like that Randy Newman song, "Mama Told Me Not to Come." My mind was reeling, it was saying to me, "WHOA, MAN, WHAT *IS* THIS?"

That was the first time I ever saw people smoking pot. The first time I'd ever *seen* pot at all was with Billy. He'd been to Mexico and brought back a fruitcake tin of joints. Pre-rolled! I don't know if they were real or not but he was very proud of himself. He goes, "This is *marijuana*."

I never did get into smoking it. It just affects me in a really bizarre way. I get completely insane! Took acid, but I couldn't smoke pot. Go figure.

By my senior year in high school my attitudes were changing. I no longer wanted to hang out with the jocks. I got bored with that. I was searching for something else and I soon found it. I started hanging out with this wild bunch of guys. Not delinquents exactly— actually they were what today would be considered the nerds. These were the kids I was performing with in the school musicals. Guys on the edge of the musician circuit. I skipped school a lot. We'd cut class and play poker instead.

I can't get no satisfaction

One of these guys promoted rock shows for all of Dallas, down at Market Hall. He would rent the building and all the kids would come to these shows. It was a bring-your-own-booze thing but nobody ever got busted. I remember he had the Kingsmen down there once, and Doug Clark & the Hot Nuts. That was my favorite band. You don't know Doug Clark & the Hot Nuts? Oh, you should find one of their albums. Real raunchy stuff—at least for those days. Like "hot nuts, hot nuts, get 'em from the peanut man, yeah yeah yeah, nuts, hot nuts, get 'em anyway you can. Well, see the man against the wall, he ain't got no nuts at all." This was considered really filthy back then.

I'd always wanted to sing, but my mother would never let me be in a rock band, or even *near* a rock band. There was a local band that wanted me to sing with them. They had a gig in Wichita Falls, which wasn't even that far from Dallas, but of course my mother said no. You're not going overnight with a rock band and that's final. At that point I was still fairly obedient. When she really put her foot down, I wouldn't defy her. But things change quickly at that age.

A little while later the performing bug bit me again. I was in a club where a local band was playing and I got up on stage and sang "Satisfaction." Not an easy song to sing, but I didn't know any better. That was my entire experience of being in a band. Did this one song, went back to my seat. Nobody applauded. My friends liked it, though.

They patted me on the back. And apparently the band liked it, too, 'cause they asked me to go out on the road with them. I hesitated about five seconds and then I said, "Sure!" I'd found a solution: Don't ask your mother.

Sorry, Mom. The lure of the spotlight was just too much for me. We had fake IDs and stuff. *Real* proud of that. We played some tiny club. In Wichita Falls, as a matter of fact.

Before that I'd sung some folk stuff with a couple of guys, been in some musicals, been in a choir. I'd sit around all day with my guitar. I'd learned all these Kingston Trio songs, and some Buffy St. Marie. But I could never figure out how to tune the damn thing. It would take me forever to get it tuned. Didn't have tuners like they do today. If they had, maybe I'd be able to play. Maybe. My songs are long enough as it is—can you imagine if I could play lead guitar? God help us.

As I got older and more into music I became more and more rebellious. One night I didn't come home. I stayed out with friends and I didn't get home till the next morning. My mom grounded me. She said, "I'm taking your driver's license away, you can't use the car." I don't know what came over me at that moment but I just lost it and I slapped her. I'm telling you, to this day that image pops into my head over and over again and it makes me crazy. I just want to go, "MOM, I'M SORRY!!!"

Godzilla

My youth was like the Wild West. If you couldn't fight, you were dead. And I got into *a lot* of fights. I got through them by going somewhere in my head—the same place I go when I'm acting. However dangerous the situation was I'd just go into this character.

When you walk on a stage, it's like football or rock-and-roll. It's the same mentality. You go into character, things take you over. Under attack, I become Godzilla. That's my totem animal, my hero. I only get scared afterward.

A guy threw a brick at me once during a fight. Concussion number ten. Hit me smack on the head with a brick. He freaked when I didn't fall down. I just kept coming at him, like Eddie the brain-dead zombie. He was so petrified that in the end he was kneeling on the ground pleading, "Please don't hurt me."

There was this fight at the Texas-Oklahoma weekend where I just sort of mutated into a movie monster on the spot, protecting my friend. These guys from Oklahoma would say, "You for Oklahoma?" All you had to say was "No, I'm for Texas," and they'd start beating up on you. That's how crazy Texas-Oklahoma weekends were.

These guys once beat up a friend of mine—apparently he had given the wrong answer. He was lying on the ground all messed up. I became Godzilla. You hurt friend? Fools! You die! I picked up these two trash cans, one in each hand, and started hitting these guys. Both hands. Left and right. They took off and ran for their lives. It was like a scene from *The Hulk*.

I once had a guy pull a gun on me, and I wasn't scared until after it was over that time, either. I said to him, "Ya know what? You better not fucking miss."

He ran away. Blew his mind. Blew *my* mind, too. When it was over, I was just shaking. I mean, it was unbelievably frightening. But at the moment, I wasn't scared at all. I was cool! That's why I never understood "Sticks and stones can break my bones but words can never hurt me." Words can do plenty, you just gotta believe 'em.

My favorite concussions

I always found it really funny that I had so many concussions and so many stupid things happened to me. My favorite is the time I got my head stuck in a steering wheel looking at Donny Anderson's girlfriend on the Texas Tech campus. I better tell you about that one.

I was driving over to the library of Texas Tech when I saw Donny Anderson's girlfriend crossing the street. She had the largest breasts that you could possibly imagine. Well, I can't take my eyes off her, and there's a car in front of me. I am paying no attention whatsoever to that car. When it stops to let somebody out, I smash right into the back of it and hit my head on the air conditioner. Another concussion!

The sixties Chevrolet I'm driving had a hole in the middle of the steering wheel, and as I slammed forward my head went right into the middle of the steering wheel and got stuck, I kid you not. My head's bleeding, I'm stuck like an idiot in my own steering wheel, and even worse a crowd has gathered. I looked pretty silly. They finally had to *cut* the steering wheel to get my head out. Concussion number—what are we up to now? Eleven, I think.

Another of my favorite concussions—because I got it in the

line of duty—was when I was playing football in my sophomore year. My head was big and the high school helmets didn't fit me. So they gave me an old Cowboys helmet with the blue stars on the side. I see the quarterback hand the ball to the fullback, this guy they call the Phenomenon, and he's coming right at me. In my mind, it's all in slow motion, and we meet like two rams—head on. Knocked us both out cold. Split that Cowboys helmet right in half. So that was another concussion. Are you keeping count? What are we up to now? Only twelve? That still leaves five unaccounted for. Let's see . . .

I was in a Corvair. I was coming back from this place across the Oklahoma border called Johnny's B29, where they would sell you beer underage. It wasn't that far, a couple of hours from Dallas maybe. You'd go into Johnny's B29, buy beer, come back. They'd sell cases of the stuff right at the border, in the middle of nowhere. That guy must have cleaned up. They had Coors there, too. There was no Coors in Texas.

I was on one of these trips out there with some friend. We were just going too fast, and the next thing you know we'd gone over the edge and rolled about ten times down the bank into the Red River—luckily there was no water in it. Your typical Texas river. I was the only one left in the car. The car was totally flat and there was beer everywhere and you could hear this loud hiss—*sssssssss*. Well, not me—I was out like a light. Concussion number—what? Thirteen?

Oh, and another time, in practice, I ran into a goalpost, got a concussion. Kind of like a one-car accident. Really stupid. Number fourteen. I can't remember them all—too many concussions!

Cars and bars and loop-de-loops

After all the years I spent looking for my father, by the time I was a teenager I was pretty experienced in the art of driving around searching for sleazy bars. Which may have prepared me for one of the only jobs I had when I was a teenager—as a bill collector.

It was the summer before I went to North Texas State, and I was working in the Fort Worth area as a collector for a finance company. They wanted me to call people up on the phone and get money from them. I couldn't do that, it was too horrible, so instead I would drive to these places and knock on the door, trying to be as polite and nice about it as possible. But it was horrendous, the worst job you could possibly have. I didn't last long. I got sick and my gallbladder had to be taken out. That's how bad that job was—it made my gallbladder operation seem like a blessing.

Fort Worth was a crazy labyrinth of streets. Having to drive around there was a nightmare. The city planner who laid out Fort Worth must have been the first person in Texas ever to have taken LSD. Owsley, the acid king, and his people probably got there early on, descended on that town, and designed the place. Because it made no sense whatsoever.

You'd be driving along looking for an address, the numbers going up and up, but you're still a few hundred numbers away from where you want to go. Then the street'll just *end*. Where'd it go? It can't just stop like that. Can it? And then you'd find that the street picked up on the other side of Fort Worth, about twenty miles away. This happened *all* the time. It would make me crazy.

Remember Chevy Chase in *European Vacation?* He's trying to get off this roundabout near Big Ben, and he's going, "Look kids, Big Ben, the Houses of Parliament, Westminster Abbey, Big Ben, the Houses of Parliament . . ." Well, that's what Fort Worth was like. They had a high, overhead loop-de-loop freeway and if you got on it and didn't get off at the right exit you'd be going around these loops absolutely forever.

the first man from mars

Anyway, there was this one black bar, it was in the Harlem of Fort Worth, and this bar was in my bill-collecting territory. God, it was awful. They told me, "You gotta go find this Bessie-Mabel. But the only time you'll find her is at night. No use going during the day, she won't be there."

So I drove up to the place. Bunch of houses and then this little grocery store next to it and then there was this bar. It was built up on cinder blocks like in South Carolina. As if it was gonna flood only it doesn't flood there.

The place was really, really, funky. Inside there was a band playing. You walked in through a screen door. At the entrance there was a bunch of tables, like a front porch with screens all around. You went through another screen door to get to the main area. There was a little four-piece band over in the corner. The place was real dark. It was night, and it was hard to make out anybody's face.

I opened the screen door and I just stood there for a moment—I was so petrified, I could barely walk. I pulled myself together, telling myself, "Meat, you gotta move." Eventually, I pulled open the inner door and took one step, and the band stopped dead in the middle of the song.

The whole place just froze. Like in a movie. Somebody *else's* movie. I'm thinking, "Oh my God!" but I don't show it.

I walked across the room, and as I walked everybody followed me with their eyes. You could actually hear my footsteps—the boards under my feet going *keeehsh keeehsh keeehsh*. I walked to the far end where the bar was.

And there, behind the bar, was this big, fat, mean-looking black woman. Without a doubt, the woman who was standing there was the woman they had described to me. A woman who could probably snap you in two if you so much as looked at her the wrong way.

"Excuse me," I asked her, "is Bessie-Mabel here?" And the woman looked back at me without batting an eye.

"No," was all she said.

I looked at her for a moment, then said, "Okay. Thanks! Just tell her that I'm from blah blah and they just wanted me to come down and, uh, *mention* that I was here."

"I'll be sure to give her the message," she says, very deadpan.

Of course I *knew* it was her, and she knew I knew it was her. There was no doubt in my mind that this was the woman, but I wasn't about to say, "You're her and I'm telling my office!" Like people do in movies just before they get killed.

It was just, "Okay, thanks!" and I turned around and walked out. Dead silence in the room on my way out. You could hear the *keeehsh keeehsh keeehsh* of my shoes all the way to the door. That screen door seemed about half a mile away. I went out and closed it behind me. Nobody moved. They just watched me, like I was the first man from Mars. It wasn't until I got off the porch and opened my car door that the band started up again.

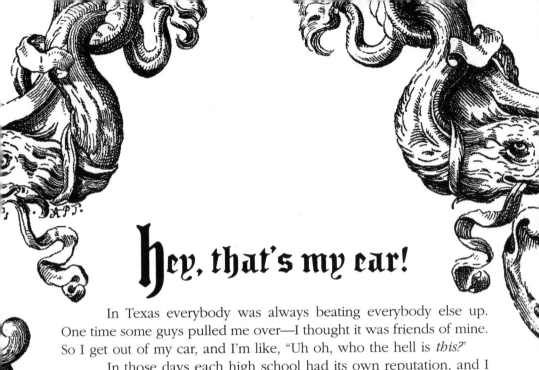

hey, that's my car!

In Texas everybody was always beating everybody else up. One time some guys pulled me over—I thought it was friends of mine. So I get out of my car, and I'm like, "Uh oh, who the hell is *this?*"

In those days each high school had its own reputation, and I knew these guys were from North Dallas High School. These were gang guys—knife-toting, gun-carrying guys! Well, just then three guys from *my* high school saw what was happening and pulled over. I was never so happy to see anybody in my life.

These three guys from my school always traveled around together in this old Dodge or Plymouth, a really cool-looking thing. Remember the cars in the movie *Streets of Fire*? That's my picture of their car.

One of 'em starts ribbing the guys who are harassing me. "You ever heard of Glenn Showers?" he says.

"Yeah, I heard of him."

"Ever heard of Bill Hartwick?" asks the other.

"Yeah, we heard of Bill Hartwick."

"Well, you're looking at them," they say. The other guys go, "Well uh, uh, uh," and get back in their car and go far, far away.

These were the kind of guys who went to Vietnam. Tough, gung-ho, let's go. They joined the Marines. Hartwick and Showers were both killed. The third one—Ekky Hudson—came back, but he had lost both legs. And it seemed this all happened in a heartbeat.

Let me tell you about North Dallas. One night coming back from somewhere we pulled into this drive-in hamburger place in another part of town. Suddenly there are shotguns going off.

People started screaming at each other. And the next thing you know, there's shotguns being fired off the roofs. *Kuush kuush kuush!* Like some TV movie, except we're in it. We're totally freaked out. The three of us crawled underneath my Buick and we stayed there until it was all over.

We used to hang out at this Jack in the Box. I actually saw two people lose *ears* at Jack in the Box places. One guy got his bit off, and the other one got it cut off by the Jack in the Box cook while trying to break up a fight. The cook grabbed the guy by the ear and accidentally cut it off with a meat cleaver he happened to be holding.

Outskirts of Dallas. Across the street from Jack in the Box was a Kmart with a big, steep hill, and I used to skateboard down it. The street had a Jack in the Box and a hot dog place and this Kmart. The Jack in the Box was a drive-through with fields all around it. There'd be tons of cars parked in the fields between the hamburger stand and the hot dog stand.

All the kids from our school would be there, and we had a *big* school. Almost four thousand people. My graduating class was twelve hundred. Lots of rich people, too. Thirty-two hundred cars in the parking lot. Thirty-seven hundred kids with thirty-two hundred cars! Tex Schramm's daughters went to this school. He ran the Dallas Cowboys. A lot of lawyers, corporate heads, and politicians. It was North Dallas, and that's where all the money was. And it kept moving on out. Now they go to other schools, but at the time that's where the money was.

Sometimes guys from some other schools would pop up and fights would constantly break out because somebody's rooting for the wrong guy. It was mind-boggling. Every weekend, people just fought. Rich *and* violent.

See, they talk about guns now and stuff, but in Texas, I mean, my father had a gun in his glove compartment. And the high school parking lot was full of pickup trucks with gunracks. Guns—shotguns!—right in the high school parking lot. I carried a baseball bat that had been sawed off and taped up with a leather strap. We'd driven nails through it.

One night we were coming back from a basketball game and pulling up at a stoplight right by Love Field, a major thoroughfare, and all of a sudden my car is completely surrounded by about eight or nine black kids and they just started swinging baseball bats at the car. We were just stopped at the light—we hadn't said anything, we hadn't done anything. We didn't even see it coming. Whoa! Next thing you know there's a bat coming from the back and from the side. I just took off. Didn't stay to discuss the situation.

Another night I was driving downtown with a friend. We're stopped at a traffic light over by the high school and a car pulls up behind us. His window's closed but the passenger-side window's rolled down, and the next thing you know, some guy comes up to the window, liquor bottle, bam! Right upside his head! Fort Worth, Texas—ya gotta love it. And we did. Usually we'd drop off our dates and head back to the Jack in the Box around two in the morning, looking for trouble, but trouble always seemed to find us.

By our last year in high school, however, we were getting more and more interested in these girls that we used to drop off. And they were getting more interested in us, or so we thought. Conveniently, we'd discovered this make-out place by a lake, the name of which for the life of me I can't remember. I've been trying for years and years and I can't even find it on the map. I was dating this girl named Rene Allen, whose father eventually became mayor of Dallas. She was the classic folk singer. Long black hair, dressed in black, black fingernails. I had a beautiful red Ford convertible at the time, the dashboard was all chrome, and at night it just lit up like a little theater. It was absolutely unbelievable. Every time we would go out to this lake, we'd sit in the car and look out at it through the windshield. But it would always end up with her saying, "Wait! Stop right there!" Every time.

boot camp

My mother wanted me to go to a Christian school, so I went first to Lubbock Christian College. It wasn't all that Christian. There was a lot of talk about religion and God and morality, but then you'd find out about faculty screwing around with underage students!

The guys I hung out with were baseball players. They didn't have a football team at the college, so I was thinking about trying to play baseball. I can hit a baseball, but I was always too big, I couldn't field. And I was scared of the ball. The photo in my high school year-book is a riot. It was supposed to be an action picture. But when they threw me the ball, I missed. So the picture is of me, my hand on my knees and the ball rolling right between my legs. Strangely enough, the only awards I ever got in baseball were for trying. Or *attendance*. And I was even more of a fish out of water at Lubbock than I'd been in high school.

I'd moved on to North Texas State when I was called for the Army physical. Okay, I said to myself, I'm gonna gain *a lot* of weight. I was already down to 225 or so, which was small for me.

Of course, *everybody's* trying to figure out how to get out of the Army—how to get a 4F or 1Y. At North Texas State we'd already had friends who were ahead of us who'd been killed in Vietnam. Glenn Showers and Bill Hartwick and others. Close friends who all joined up together and all ended up dead together over there.

Before the Army physical, I did my best to get out of the draft. I gained sixty-eight pounds in four and a half weeks. That just goes to show you the willpower involved! But when I went to the Army physical, they knew. The first thing they asked me was, "How much weight have you gained recently?" They could tell, and they started giving me a hard time. Can you imagine what these guys went through every day? People acting crazy. Doing this, doing that—everybody wanting out. They must have gone totally out of their minds dealing with kids who were doing everything in the world to get out of the Army. Everybody had some scam going.

Okay. So I go into the physical—they're gonna check your heart and all that and everything's going fine. Then comes the eye test. There wasn't the usual chart on the wall that you look at with one eye covered and read the line. It was a machine that you looked into. So I put my head down, and he says, "Okay, read line three." I'm looking, but I don't see lines.

There were probably nine hundred people with me at the physical, and it seemed like nobody wanted to go to Vietnam. And they're all *talking* about it. "Oh, I've got letters from the doctor, I've got this, I've got that." Everybody walking around with letters and blah blah blah. And here's this guy, some sergeant, saying, "Read the line."

"Don't see the line."

"All right, son, no more fooling around. Just read the line."

"Yessir." Pause. "Don't see the line."

"Move out of the way," he says. Now he's getting mad.

"Son, put you head back down on that viewer and read that third line." I put my head back down on the viewer, but I don't see a thing. Nothing. Just white. That's all I see.

But as I'm raising my head, my eyes divert up, and when they do I see the letters. So I'm trying to explain this to him: "I was looking down and you have to look up. I'm sorry." That type of thing.

"Just . . . read . . . the . . . line," he says. "The fourth one."

"Yessir."

"That's much better," he says. Then he puts in this color wheel thing and he says: "Tell me what you see."

"Colored dots."

"I *know* you see colored dots, but what do you see *in* the dots?"

"Nothing."

He takes it out. Puts it back in. Tell me what you see. Dots. Takes it out, puts it in. Oh, a star! Okay, you see a star in there. Out, in. What do you see? Dots. WHAT DO YOU SEE *IN* THE DOTS, YOU SON OF A BITCH? Nothing.

Now, he stands up, he's enraged. He tries to *pick me up*, and he's screaming at me. "Don't think you're getting out of this man's army! We're gonna take you, that's right. You're going to boot camp and be a bombadier. If you're colorblind, you can see through camouflage. Even guys like you are useful in the army."

He's yelling, he's red in the face, he's seriously losing it. Finally, these two other guys come up wondering what's going on. "THIS GUY! First he did this, then he did that, blah blah blah blah blah."

"Okay, kid," they say, "end of the line." So now I'm back at the end of the line. And I wait and I wait and I wait. Come back to the same guy. "Okay," he says, "tell me what you see."

"Dots."

He stands up, face all bulging out. He's swearing a blue streak at me.

Same two guys come up. Chip 'n' Dale. "What's going on?"

"He will NOT read . . . read . . . read—" He's sputtering.

"Son," say Chip 'n' Dale, "this is not a joke, tell us what—"

"Dots."

"Are you colorblind?" one of them asks me.

"Yessir," I say meekly. And my guy, the sergeant, goes loony.

"But he didn't *ask* me," I say, at which point my guy goes completely berserk. They had to take him away, I'm not kidding. I felt bad for the guy. I thought he was going to have a coronary.

Next they take my blood.

"Do you have any problem taking blood?"

"Yessir! I do not like needles, whenever I get blood taken I faint."

They take my blood anyway, and when I don't faint it pisses them off in some way. Now *they* hate me, too. They had guys standing there ready to catch me.

"Are you just *doing* this?"

"Nosir, nosir." Finally they take me in to the doctor, and I have letters—*lots* of letters. I have letters about shoulders, I have letters about concussions.

"So I hear you've been giving us a lot of trouble today."

"Nosir, I haven't been."

"Well, that's not what they've been telling me," he says. "What's this about a trick shoulder?"

"Well sir, this shoulder comes out."

"We can put you in an Army hospital and fix that right up. How bad is it?"

"Comes out all the time."

"Oh yeah?"

"Yessir, I can make it come out right now, but you're going to have to put it back in."

He takes one long, hard look at me and says, "That won't be necessary." Stamp! "1Y—we'll see you in four months."

I finally got the letter two years later, telling me to go to the draft. I ignored it. For years, every time I came back into the country I thought for sure they were going to haul me off. I was such a mess, maybe they eventually made me 4F.

That was one of my favorite things ever, going to the Army physical. People asked me how I got out of it and I said, "They thought I was crazy, can you imagine that?" Seriously, between me and that sergeant, who was the crazy one?

The guy had a nervous breakdown over me—some poor kid who weighs three hundred pounds and can't see the line. He was foaming at the mouth when they took him away—just because I couldn't see the squirrel on a color wheel. I'm telling you, *that* guy shoulda been 4F.

PART 2

shakespeare,
grand funk railroad,
eddie the brain-dead zombie,
and general ulysses s. grant

Í'll tell you why i left texas

I barely recognized her. My mother was a big lady, just like my dad was big, and here in this hospital bed was the body of an emaciated woman. At first I thought I must be in the wrong room, but when I got closer I saw it was my mother. The cancer had just eaten her up.

It was the spring of 1967, and I was still at North Texas State. Mom had been ill for years, but suddenly she was much worse. I hadn't seen her in a few weeks. I walked into her room and I was devastated. She was in a plastic oxygen tent, asleep. She didn't even know I was there.

I couldn't deal with it—I practically lost my mind. I went home and packed a bag. In the process of rummaging around I found my father's credit card. I went to the bank, took out some money, grabbed a guitar and one suitcase, and headed for the airport. When I got there I looked up on the departure board for the next plane to anywhere.

I had no idea where—I was just going. The next flight out of Dallas was to Los Angeles on Braniff Airways. I went up to the counter to buy a ticket. The girl who sold it to me was one of the girls I'd taken to the prom. Paulette Ferrar.

"Oh," she said. "It's *you!*"

"Guess so," I said, the words reverberating in the air. It was very bizarre. I hardly knew who was speaking.

"Can you get me on this flight to LA?" I asked.

"Sure can!" she said with a big smile, pretending she wasn't talking to a crazy person.

I got on the plane, but I had no idea what I was doing. I sure didn't know anybody where I was going. When I got to LA, I picked up my guitar and suitcase and just sat on one of those cement benches outside the baggage claim. I sat there for the longest time. After a while I started to realize what I'd done.

Up to this point I had been going on mad energy but as soon as I stopped I began to ask myself. "Meat, what are you doing? You can't just sit here forever."

"You're right—I'll just turn around and go back."

Then I sat around some more. Hmm. Maybe I'll get in a taxi and go to the Sunset Strip—having, of course, no idea where that was. Or what.

So I get in a taxi and tell the driver, "Sunset Strip!"

"Where, kid?"

"You know, Sunset Strip, the place where everybody—"

"Yeah, yeah," he says, "but *where* on Sunset?"

I was tempted to say, "77 Sunset Strip," but I just said, "Take me where the hippies are."

So he dropped me off across the street from the Whisky a Go-Go and, believe me, I was in absolute shock. I'm standing on this corner wearing a sport jacket and cowboy boots. In Dallas my hair was considered long—they called me "hair god" because my hair would curl out from under my football helmet, but here on the Strip I looked really straight. I mean *really* straight. There were guys with hair down to their waists.

meat loaf TO HELL AND BACK

I'd been standing on the corner about ten minutes when I saw a guy crossing the street with a *huge* Afro. The size of this Afro would be the equivalent of, say, having a tumbleweed on the top of your head. A *giant* tumbleweed. As he walked, I swear, the thing moved by itself, as if it were lifting the guy across the street.

I was flabbergasted. All these people, all this *leather*. And beads. This was ripe sixties. Hippie hippie heaven, and the state police all over. I'm standing there thinking, "What in the *world*?"

By eleven o'clock at night the place was mobbed. Like being at the concession stand at a World Series game.

I start walking down the street, and I run straight into Don Burns, a guitar player from Dallas. I had met him only two or three times, and just knew him as a good guitar player. At least I *think* he was. He may have been terrible, but I didn't know one from the other. To me the guy seemed just unbelievably good. I used to sit there going, *"Wow, man!"*

And there he is, right on the corner of Sunset and Larrabee.

"Hey Meat, what time is it?" he asks me like we'd just seen each other that morning.

"Uh, I don't know."

"Well, where are you staying?"

"Uh, I don't know." And I didn't. I barely knew who I *was*.

"Well, look here," he says, "I got a two-bedroom apartment right around the corner on Doheny and the guy that was sharing it with me just left today. You can stay there." This was the sixties; stuff like that happened all the time.

# I lose my mom and my dad tries to kill me

I could no longer afford to pay my half of the rent on Don Burns's apartment and I moved out. After I ran out of the credit card money, I wound up as a bouncer at a teenage nightclub on Ventura Boulevard in Encino. I slept in the back of the club. By day, it was a psychedelic shop that sold black light posters. At night, it became a teenage nightclub. Local Valley musicians hung out in the courtyard. Long gone now—they built a skyscraper on top of it.

The courtyard had a gate to it, and in the psychedelic shop itself there were different rooms where they sold stuff, not actual drugs—although I'm sure they did that, too. They had four or five little stores within the store itself: In one room they sold hippie clothing, in another, pipes and papers, and in the back they served food and drinks. They had picnic benches in the courtyard where you could sit and eat.

The place was mobbed with kids from seven o'clock to midnight, kids as young as eleven and twelve on up to twenty. Every once in a while you'd get some famous rock bands coming by, so over the course of working there I met a lot of musicians. Guys from the Electric Prunes and Iron Butterfly would come in. Not the Neil Youngs and the David Crosbys, or the Roger McGuinns. Those guys were over in another part of town. But Canned Heat showed up one night. And a Valley band called the Yellow Pages.

I was there all the time because I lived there. When they closed up I'd be the night watchman. This didn't go on very long; I couldn't have been there more than a month.

One morning, I woke up and heard the highway patrol outside asking if anybody knew so-and-so. I couldn't hear what the name was. It was early in the morning and someone getting ready to open the store. Nobody there knew my real name. "No no no, there's no one here by that name," they said.

I went out and asked what they wanted. They told me the police were looking for this Marvin Aday about a family matter. The minute I heard my name, I knew my mother had died.

I had to get back to Dallas but I was totally broke. The kids at that store got together a collection and raised enough money for me to go home. The ticket was a hundred and something dollars, and they collected $330. And I went home that very night, taking nothing with me except the clothes I had on.

I remember very little about going back home. I remember landing and my Aunt Mary picking me up. Initially, I went out and stayed with one of my cousins. At the funeral home I saw the casket through the doorway, but I wouldn't go into the room.

I've blacked out the whole thing, but apparently what I did at the funeral service was pull my mother out of the casket and say they couldn't have her. I actually lifted her into my arms, and people were horrified.

The whole thing totally destroyed me. I decided to head right back to California, but in the three or four days before I left, my dad tried to kill me with a knife.

What happened was I found out that my mother left me money, and that my dad was trying to get it. So I went to a judge, and the lawyer explained that my dad was an alcoholic and gambled. The judge got the he's-a-minor thing waived so I could get the money. Ironically, I would soon squander it all away.

My dad was in very bad shape. I had never seen him so lost. He'd started drinking again and he wasn't the kind of alcoholic that stayed at home and passed out on the couch. He was gone, good-bye. I don't know if he was with other women or what. I don't know what he was doing but he would be gone for four or five days.

I'd see him come into the house. I don't know if he even knew where he'd been. I don't think there was any plan; he just went out on these binges and got drunk. Sort of like Ray Milland in *The Lost Weekend*. That was my dad *every* weekend.

He'd get into fights. I remember seeing him out in the alley in back of our house trying to get home, and he was really beat up bad. Seeing him come in the front door, blood everywhere from being in some barroom brawl. Divorce didn't seem to be an option in our little corner of the world, but that kind of stress will kill you, and I think it did. Killed him, and my mother, too.

He stopped drinking for a while and things were a little better, especially when my mother got sick. Eventually he ran away and went back to drinking. I couldn't deal with her being sick so I ran away. I ran away from her, too. I was still a kid, I was confused. I don't know if he was home when my mother died. I know I wasn't there. I'll blame myself forever for that. After her death my father disappeared. He ran away, and totally lost his mind.

One night shortly after the funeral I was sitting in my parents' house with Billy Slocum. Just hanging out at the dining room table. In walks my dad and he's drunk. And violent. "Get all these whores out of here!" he's screaming. Of course there's nobody in the house but me and Billy.

Billy got up. He could see my dad was out of his mind. Under my breath I said, "Billy, you better get out of here." I jumped up and went into my bedroom and shut the door. The next thing I know my father's standing in the doorway with a butcher knife in his hand. His eyes are blank, as if he'd been hypnotized. I knew he was very disturbed so my first thought was, "Oh my God, he's going to kill himself." But when he walked toward me and raised the knife above his head, it took a split second for me to realize, "God, he's going to kill *me*."

I backed up as he came toward me, tripping and falling backward onto the bed. In a panic I realized there was no way out—the bed was against the wall. He put both hands on the handle of the knife and brought it down. As I rolled to the end of the bed and dropped to the floor I could hear the knife ripping through the bedding into the mattress. I looked up at him. There was no one there behind his eyes.

Believe it or not, Dad was bigger than me. And stronger. He could always throw me around. When I was about twelve he threw me through a screen door. He just picked me up and threw me— kaaaaa!—right through it. When he put the knife into that bed, he really was trying to *kill* me. To him, the screen door incident was just good, clean fun.

I crouched by the bed. It was a moment of pure terror. He pulled the knife out of the bed and turned and looked down at me on the floor. There was no way I could slip past him. I was trapped. With some kind of crazy energy, I just lunged at him. He stumbled into the dresser. I ran out the door into the hallway. He came after me. He dropped the knife—he'd decided to kill me with his bare hands.

He hit me in the face, and I reeled back against the wall. I kicked him away. We had this huge fight that ended up in the living room. We must have gone all the way down the hall through the family room out into the living room. It was a knockdown, drag-out kind of thing. I just kept going at him and he kept hitting me.

He threw me across the living room and I crashed into a lamp. I got up and he was still coming at me. I hit him in the face. He lost his balance and went tumbling back across a barrel-type chair. I think he broke a couple of ribs. He didn't get up right away and I just ran straight out of the house.

Why he tried to kill me, I don't know. Maybe he was feeling guilty about my mother—and I *looked* like her. As soon as I got out the door the full horror of it struck me. My own father had tried to *kill* me. Not "my father didn't *love* me." He actually wanted me dead.

I went out that front door and never came back. All I had on was a T-shirt and shorts, no shoes. I walked over to Billy's house and called my Aunt Mary and that was it. I never looked back.

I was completely freaked out. I just wanted to find a dark corner and hide from the world. After I got my inheritance, I rented an apartment down in the Turtle Creek area of Dallas. Then I bought a bunch of food, parked the car in the garage, and stayed in that apartment for three and a half months. I never left. Never once went out.

I have no idea what I did for that whole period of time. I've blanked on the whole thing, possibly to preserve my sanity. This entire time my friends and family were looking everywhere for me. Billy was the one who finally found me. He knew I'd had an apartment in that area before, so he drove around till he found my car parked in a garage down some alley.

It was a studio apartment over the garage, just a sofa bed in the living room. When Billy opened the door the sofa bed was pulled out; there were cans and wrappers and cartons strewn everywhere. The kitchen area was piled high with garbage and dirty dishes.

I vaguely remembered saying to myself at one point, probably a few months earlier, "One of these days, I've really got to clean this place up." When I opened the door, Billy took one look around and said, "Come on, we're leaving." Didn't even ask, "How are you?"

Is there a problem, officer?

I wound up staying with my cousin Camille and her husband, who raised turkeys. She said, "Meat, you best stay here a while until you get yourself together. Just think about taking care of the turkeys."

My job was looking after those ten turkeys and picking pecans. They had big pecan trees, and part of their business was bagging pecans. So I bagged pecans and fed the turkeys. I was helping out with the kids. It was kinda calm, actually. I bought myself a '65 Chevy with that money and at some point I just got in it and took off for California.

As I was going through this town in New Mexico I noticed a cop was following me and wondered what was wrong. Eventually the cop pulled me over and said, "Did you see me behind you?"

"Oh yeah," I said. I knew I wasn't speeding 'cause I'd seen him and was going slow. He'd been following me through the whole town.

"Just where are you headed?"

"Well, I'm coming from Dallas and I'm going to California 'cause my friends are there and—"

"Can you tell me why you just ran all those red lights?"

"What red lights?"

"Buddy," he says, "you just ran I don't know how many red lights."

"No," I said, "they were green. Sir."

"Son," he says, "they were red."

I was trying to be polite and eventually it rolled around to where I was explaining to him, look, red is on the top and green is on the bottom.

And he smiled and said, "Son, in New Mexico red is at the bottom and green is at the top. "

"Ah!"

"Are you colorblind?"

"I am now!"

He just laughed and laughed.

this drummer's got no fingers

I moved to LA and found a place to live. I remember spending Christmas alone, which was horrifying; the worst. I was alone, I had the flu, and I was in some lousy apartment on Ventura Boulevard. There were reindeer on the roof of the building but the snow was Styrofoam and the Christmas trees were pink. Christmas is the worst time of year when you are depressed, but being in LA gave the whole thing a grotesque glow.

When I finally got out of my funk I started going up to the Balboa Youth Center and sitting in with different bands. From hanging out there I found out about Big Brother, the Blues Project, Jimi Hendrix, the Yardbirds, all those bands. Nobody in Texas knew about them yet.

I learned all these Janis Joplin songs from listening to records, and after a while I could do a pretty good "Piece of My Heart." When I did the Yardbirds' "Smokestack Lightning" kids would go crazy. People started taking me seriously. This guy from the Electric Prunes said his brother knew somebody who owned a little studio, so we decided we'd go into the studio and record three songs. One of them was called "Animal." A crazy little thing I'd written in high school. "A-n-i-m-a-l, I'm an animal." Stupid lyrics, but I could growl as good as Howlin' Wolf by then. Or so I thought.

Another song I'd written was called "Deep River Blues," about the, uh, deep river blues. Sounded good. Never knew what it meant.

I went into the studio with Rick Bozzo, a bass player I'd met in Encino; and a guitar player named Gary Spagnaia. We didn't have a drummer. There was a big drum store next door, and I sent the guys over to see if they could find a drummer and they did. His name was Peter Woodman and when I went to shake his hand, he had no fingers. Okay, I now had a drummer with no fingers. I looked at the bass player. There's a drum set out 'cause it goes with the room, and Woodman goes up there and starts to play. "This guy's got no fingers," I'm saying, "what are you doing?" Then I hear him playing in the background. He really *could* play, so he became the drummer. Played with us for three years.

That was the first band, Meat Loaf Soul. Woodman was the drummer and he was good—he knew about arrangements and things. We got some tracks down and I went in to do the vocals. I had never been in a studio before. I started to sing and right off I hit this one big note and everything shut off. I think I blew a fuse. Took the whole board out. They must really have been impressed with that because my first day in the studio, I was offered three recording contracts. I'm not kidding. That's when I finally figured out that I was on to something.

Green & Stone, who were the Buffalo Springfield's producers, offered me a contract; an A&R guy from A&M Records made me an offer and I got another one from the guy who owned the studio. I turned them all down. I didn't even know who Green & Stone *were*. I didn't know anything. I knew who Jimi Hendrix and Janis Joplin were, 'cause I had the tapes. And I'd met the Electric Prunes back in Encino. I knew who Iron Butterfly was because they would sit up there and play at the Balboa Youth Center, and of course I knew who Canned Heat was. I was a huge Buffalo Springfield fan, but I had no idea that Green & Stone were their producers. If I had known that, I would have signed with them in a heartbeat.

ᚣou wanna meet a beach boy?

I'm driving around down on Sunset one day and I pick up this guy hitchhiking.

"Where are you heading?" I ask.

"I'm only going up the hill," he says. "I'm staying at the Beach Boys' house. You wanna meet a Beach Boy?" He's really into name dropping.

"There's some other people up there, too. Neil Young—you wanna meet Neil Young?"

So I gave the guy a ride up the hill. When we got up to the house there were a bunch of musicians there, but nobody I'd ever heard of. And there was no Beach Boy there, although it actually was Dennis Wilson's house. A twelve-bedroom log cabin with a swimming pool in the shape of California.

I hung around for a while and the hitchhiker said he'd tell me my fortune, although I didn't really need to hear it because the world was going to end very shortly. I wondered if I'd have time to get my singing career off the ground first.

He told me that I'd been a cat in a former life and that I'd never have any money.

"Gee, thanks," I said.

Then he told me that Kirilian photography is proof that they had color TV in Atlantis.

"Absolute proof!" He paused. "Do you think the false prophet Richard Nixon can end the war in Vietnam?"

"Uh, no?"

"I am Abraxas, baby, the son of Darkness, and I will lay waste all the J. C. Penneys from Rhode Island to Pasadena."

"Absolutely," I said, backing out of the room. A few years later I saw his picture in the paper. His name was Charles Manson. I never did get to meet a Beach Boy.

Under the boardwalk

As Meat Loaf Soul we got our first gig up at Huntington Beach. At the Cave. Opening for a Brit band called Them—Van Morrison was the lead singer.

We did "Smokestack Lightning," and me being who I am, I wanted theatrics. So we decided that for "Smokestack Lightning" we'd put up smoke. So we put up these, I don't know, *smoke things*. We made way too much of the stuff and they had to clear everybody out of the club. Management was not too thrilled.

One night while I was playing at the Cave I walked out across the road to the end of this pier and decided to jump off into the ocean. I have no idea why. All of a sudden there I was. I'm looking down and a voice says, "You don't want to do that."

I stopped, turned around, and saw an old lady standing there.

"She still loves you," she told me. "She still loves you, and it's not your fault."

I just looked at this lady; I didn't say a word. I watched her walk away, right out of my line of vision. I stood there for a second, then I said, "Whoa!"

It couldn't have been more than a minute before I turned around—and it's a long pier—but when I looked back there was no one there. To this day, I think it was my mother. Now I have never told that story to anyone. Just to Leslie, my wife.

I walked off the pier down to the beach. I couldn't figure it out. There had been no time for this woman to get off this pier, 'cause it was just a straight wooden pier. It would have taken you three or

four minutes just to go down it, and it's wide open at the street so even if she'd gotten to the end and turned this way or that way or gone straight, you'd see her.

Did I see this woman? Did I not see this woman? And what the hell was I doing at the end of this pier? I was a strange sight. I weighed about 310 pounds, and I was wearing a big yellow Nehru shirt—I looked like a giant bumble bee, sitting on a beach. I don't even like sand.

The band came down asking, "Where have you been?" and "Who're you talking to?"

"Nobody."

"What happened to you? Did you drop acid or something? C'mon, we gotta get back to the club, we're on next."

"I'm sorry, guys, I was, uh, *hot*—the club was really hot." I went back and did the show. Then went home and tried not to think about it.

Eventually we got on the bill out at Cal State Northridge. We were the first act up. The headliners were Renaissance, Taj Mahal, and Janis Joplin and Big Brother. That's where I met Janis. I thought I recognized her from Splash Day down in Galveston. I went over to her—she was drinking Southern Comfort right out of the bottle—and I asked her, "Did you ever sing down there in Galveston? 'Cause I think I might have seen you there. Were you wearing white go-go boots?"

She looked me right in the eye and said, "Don't ever say that again, motherfucker!" So, you know, I assume it *was* her. That was my one conversation with Janis.

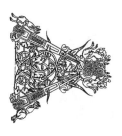

they're all crazy!

We decided to go to Michigan with Meat Loaf Soul. Rick Bozzo, me, our fingerless drummer, Peter Woodman, and his wife, Sue. Pete had been in a really popular band back in '65 called the Bossmen—Dick Wagner had been in that band, too, and went on to play with Alice Cooper and cowrite all those songs with him. Pete encouraged us to try our luck in the Motor City.

"Let's go back to Michigan; I bet I can get us a lot of dates, just, you know, on the fact that I was in the Bossmen. Hey, I might even be able to find us a sponsor so we can go buy some new equipment."

And he did. He convinced the wife of the chairman of Dow Chemical to buy equipment! We bought a Sun amplifier, Sun speakers, and a Sun PA system. We had Sun everything. Along with new drums, new organs, and lights.

We had a U-Haul trailer and a '59 Buick. That's how we got around. Nobody else could pack that trailer the way I did. We had lights—four or five tiny lights. I used to work them (three little buttons) with my feet. I did the sound, too.

We were looking good. Then the name game started. From Meat Loaf Soul to Popcorn Blizzard to the Floating Circus. All because we could never keep the lead guitar players. They'd say, "Well, I might join, but, man, you guys gotta change the name. I'm not playing in a band called—" well, whatever we were called.

Lead guitar players are nuts. Back then I didn't know how to deal with them. At all. Lead guitar players are in their own world, all the time. A good one is always inside his guitar; nothing else exists for him.

Our band went through so many guitar players that we eventually said to hell with it, we'll go out as a power trio—organ, bass, drums, and me. As the Floating Circus I wore a tuxedo and went barefoot on stage. The drummer dressed like a clown. Clown makeup and clown costume (way ahead of Insane Clown Posse!) and the bass player dressed like an Indian (way ahead of the . . . errr . . . Village People). Sue had on a swan outfit. A swan, a clown, and an Indian— I was the ringmaster.

We opened for everybody from Dr. John to Sun Ra. That Floating Circus band opened for everybody. The Fugs. We opened for the Who two or three times. That's when I met Roger Daltrey and all those guys. I saw Daltrey ten years later in 1978 at a music industry convention in Miami. I'm in the bathroom taking a piss and he comes in and says, "You're Meat Loaf, ain't you? You know wot, man? I remember you from 1968. I came down to your dressing room after the show and we had a chat? You was really good, mate."

I was blown away. I couldn't believe that he remembered. Of course, back in those days everybody used to watch everybody else, used to go out into the house actually. At the Grandee Ballroom, you had no choice—there was no place else to go. No backstage, no dressing room. So if you weren't on, you really *had* to be in the house. It didn't matter who the hell you were, you'd sit out there on those velvet couches with everybody else.

We were on the bill at the Grandee Ballroom the night that the Stooges first played. The Stooges, who later became Iggy and the Stooges, were nothing more than the road crew for the MC5. They were all roadies, and none of them could play a note. Eventually the guitar player worked up an E chord and the bass player just slapped the E string and the drummer beat on the drums. Then Iggy came out, shirtless and shoeless in these really tight pants. He was just blathering. Nobody could understand a word he was saying. Out of the blue, he jumped into the audience with a pie in his hand, looking for a victim. Then he jumped back up on stage. That was the act. It cracked me up, just hilarious.

We played the Ann Arbor Blues Festival once with Iggy. I went over to talk to him and this may have been one of only two conversations I've ever had with him.

"We got *songs!*" he whispered. He always spoke really softly. "We learned *three* chords. E, A, and D." He was so excited. Come to think of it, whenever I saw him, Iggy always had a big smile on his face. You never knew whether he was really stoned or not, but he was definitely out there. And he was happy. *"Hey, Meat, how are you?"* he'd whisper. *"Yeah, man, we learned three chords."*

The first time we opened for the MC5 was somewhere in Michigan. I walked out on stage to put our equipment up—they'd already done their sound check, and their amps were covered in American flags and psychedelic stuff. They had massive equipment, *walls* of equipment. The sound was pure white noise. I loved Wayne Kramer, the lead guitarist. He'd do these solos and he'd spin around and wrap himself completely in his guitar cord, you know, those curly ones, like a phone cord? He'd wrap it around himself until it was completely taut and then spin out of it. These guys were very theatrical. Rob Tyner, the lead singer of the MC5, used to come sliding across the stage, screaming, "Kick out the jams, motherfuckers!" as his opening thing. They had this preacher guy introduce them with "PEOPLE, ARE YOU READY?" I always loved that, and the way they dressed in glitter outfits with American flags in their hands.

We played a lot of gigs but we were getting absolutely nowhere with the record companies. We got turned down by every single record company. I found this very frustrating and puzzling. I'd gone from being offered three record contracts the first day I was in the business to not being able to get *any* record contract for two and a half years. Welcome to show business.

four and a half hours with live hogs!

One night, the Grateful Dead played on the same bill as us. Of course, I had no idea who the Grateful Dead were. Heard the name, but I had no idea what they did.

Well, the night before, their equipment had gotten snowed in, so they came to us and asked if they could use our equipment.

Yeah, sure. I was gonna watch them anyway, so what's the difference? How did I know they were gonna play for four hours and thirty-five minutes? The same song!

They started and never stopped. There were several points where it looked like they were going to finish, but they just kept playing. Nothing stopped them. And I'm looking at the clock. They'd probably gone on at ten-thirty or something and I figured they'd be off soon and I'd started packing up, 'cause I wouldn't let anybody else pack our equipment. We were there all night.

And they had all these hogs running around the building. Real hogs running around in the Grandee Ballroom. The Hog Farm followed them around in those days.

The Technicolor swine were rampaging through the Grandee like hairy Huns sacking Rome. They knocked over the monitors, chewed the Naugahyde couches. Egging them on was Wavy Gravy himself in a stars-and-stripes suit, riding a fine six-hundred-pound pig and singing "The Battle Hymn of the Republic."

With a little help from my friend

We were scheduled to play at a festival in Pontiac, Michigan. The headliner was called the Grease Band. The MC5 is on the form, Ted Nugent and the Amboy Dukes are on, Dick Wagner and the Frost are on. These are all huge bands in this area. And I'm thinking, "Who is the Grease Band? And why are they headlining?"

Our organ was a monster, a C3. It came from a church, and it was solid wood. A B3 weighs like three hundred pounds, a C3 weighs seven hundred and something pounds. So I'm moving this around by myself most of the time, with these dollies. I'm able to do it. Just. At one of our gigs, this guy comes up to me. Friendly type, thick English accent—a roadie, I'm thinking. And the first thing out of his mouth is "Ooh, I bet it ain't easy shiftin' weight like that, mate."

"Yeah," I say, "it's a brute." I figure he's talking about the organ.

"No, *you*, mate," he says. "Quite a corporation you got there, innit?"

What a way to open a conversation. I'm looking at him a little oddly, trying to think what to come back with.

"Aw, don't be like that," he says. "I usta weigh wot you do, can you credit it? Yeah, mate, I usta to weigh about eighteen stone meself. But I've lost weight now."

"I'm very happy for you," I say.

"You was bloody good up there tonight."

"Oh thanks."

"Listen," he says, "we're 'aving a problem wit our organ and I was wondering if you minded if we used yours?"

Immediately my mind went back to the time we'd lent our equipment to the Grateful Dead. So I looked at him a little skeptically. "How long are you guys going to play?"

"Oh an hour, an hour and a half."

So I help this Brit roadie take the organ out and set it up. The show starts, the MC comes out, "Put your hands together for . . . the Grease Band!" It's Leon Russell and company. He's playing the organ and singing and I'm still thinking, "They're the headliners? I don't get this."

They finish the first song and out walks the guy I thought was the roadie, my diet counselor. They go into another song, and the roadie walks up to the microphone and starts to sing. My heavens, it's Joe Cocker. I'm mesmerized. The man is unbelievable, contorting himself around the stage, doing all this wild spastic "dancing," and singing in that croaky voice of his. "Oh my God! Oh my God!" was all I could say. I started following him everywhere after that. Whenever he was playing, I'd go see him. I went to see Joe Cocker more than anyone other than the MC5. And maybe the Buffalo Springfield.

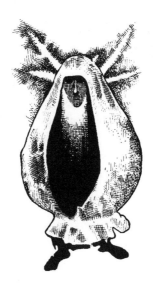

the worst advice i ever gave

In the late sixties in Michigan the big local band was the Pack. It consisted of Donny Brewer, Craig Frost, and Mark Farner. Craig Frost was probably the best organ player, other than Lee Michaels, I've ever seen. Donny Brewer was a great drummer and Mark Farner was a good bass player. But what Mark Farner did best was sing.

They were working steadily as the Pack, but for whatever reason, they had just slowly slid down from being headliners to second on the bill. Sometimes they were going on second or even first at the Grandee Ballroom.

Things had really gone downhill by this point for the Pack, and after one last, disastrous gig, they chucked it in. They'd gone to Boston to open for Gary Puckett and the Union Gap, and this turned out to be the last straw, one of the most humiliating gigs I've ever heard of. Gary Puckett was an egomaniac, and what he put them through I've never heard of anyone doing to another act, to this day. Gary Puckett should be punched in the nose. My opinion.

Even though the Pack was the opening act, Puckett refused to allow them to set their equipment on the same stage with him. He made them set up on the *floor*. And that's where they had to play, down on the floor with the audience milling around. This was so demoralizing that after that gig the band just broke up.

So Mark Farner and Donny Brewer decided they were going to put together a trio. They were rehearsing in Flint, Michigan, at the YMCA, and looking for a bass player. They called up Rick Bozzo, the bass player in our band, 'cause Rick could play. He was really good, and they wanted him in their group in the worst way.

"Listen, Rick," they said, "we're putting together this power trio, and we'd really like for you to play bass."

Rick was unsure what to do, so he came to me and said, "Look, Mark Farner called me up and wants me to go join his new

meat loaf TO HELL AND BACK

band." And I looked at him and I said, "Rick, we're doing really good right now. We're making good money. We're finally able to breathe a little."

Before we only had one car between all of us. Now he had a car, I had a car. I'd just bought a Mustang. We were able to move out into our own places instead of all living together. I had an apartment, he had an apartment. I said, "We're right on the verge—I know we're going to get a record deal. Look, I know how great Mark is, but these guys aren't going to do anything. Look what happened to the Pack— they broke up."

The long and the short of it is that I talked Rick Bozzo out of joining Grand Funk Railroad. I still cringe every time I think of it.

The only thing that Rick ever said to me about it was after our band had broken up. Rick and I were back in California, and we were putting together another band. One day we were driving down Sunset Boulevard, and there was this giant billboard of Mark Farner, Donny Brewer, and the bass player, Mel Schacher. Just giant heads of these guys, the size of Mount Rushmore. I'm driving, and we come up on this thing, and I say, "Wow, look at that."

And Rick just looks at me, and he goes, "Coulda been me." That was the only thing he ever said about it.

96 tears

By 1969, the Meat Loaf Soul/Popcorn Blizzard/Floating Circus band had broken up. Eventually, Rick Bozzo and I packed it in in Michigan and came back to California. We fooled around with different musicians, mostly out in the valley—Sherman Oaks—'cause that's the people he knew.

I lived in a house with some people at Oak Park and hung out with a guy named Barney who lived up the street from Linda Ronstadt in Franklin Canyon. She had this old house that she eventually moved out of. Some friends of mine rented it, which was a big thrill for me. Just to be in Linda Ronstadt's ex-house. She wasn't that famous yet, but I was a big fan of hers.

Basically, I was just hanging out in LA. I don't have a clue what I was doing for money. Still had a little left over from the band, I guess.

And I had a lot of odd jobs, but definitely the weirdest was looking after Question Mark. ? and the Mysterians had had a monster hit with "96 Tears" in 1966. A cult classic. What they'd been doing for the last three years, however, was something of a mystery. Question Mark was a bit of a mystery himself.

He and the rest of the Mysterians came from that same area in Michigan that I'd just left: Midland Bay City, Saginaw. Popcorn Blizzard actually cut a couple of demos in the same studio where they had recorded "96 Tears."

The organ player was like twelve years old. And Question Mark at that time, in the sixties, was around thirty-six years old, at least. He *looked* ancient. Pete Woodman was friends with these guys and he knew Question Mark was a real handful. So when they came to LA to play gigs at Gazzari's on the Strip, they naturally want to keep him from getting unhinged. They hired me for the two and a half weeks to be Question's bodyguard. To be his minder. They saw how big I was and figured I could control him. Wrong.

According to the sources around the band, he sniffed glue. I never personally saw him do it, but he had a lot of it. You know that airplane glue that came in tan tubes? Well, let's just say he had lots of tubes of glue and no model airplanes. They tried to keep him under control but said he'd sneak out of the hotel and go buy that darn airplane glue. Then back to the hotel to trash rooms, break beds and TVs, and throw things out the window.

They put me in the room right next to him. I never got any sleep. I was up twenty-four hours a day with this guy. He was fine during the day when everybody was moving around and stuff was going on. And on the days of the shows he seemed to be okay.

He never *said* anything. Basically he was just led around from place to place in his wraparound sunglasses. I don't remember ever having a conversation with him. If he did talk, he spoke Spanish. So that was another reason I didn't understand him.

I had a key to his room and at night I would listen at his door every hour on the hour just to make sure there was nothing going on. One night I heard strange noises coming from Question's room. I

unlocked the door and went in. He was prowling the room and muttering terrible curses at some unseen demon. Broken chair, broken lamp. I grabbed him and took him into my room. He'd gone completely feral—he tried to bite me. I threw him on the bed and called the Mysterians and together we succeeded in subduing him. Kinda. I mean, he tried smoking pot to calm himself down but only succeeded in throwing up. He was a mess. I thought *I* was a mess. It's a weird kinda self-help cure. Take care of someone in worse shape than you are.

fifty dollars plus tips

My friend Barney had a job parking cars at the theater where *Hair* was playing. One day he tells me somebody has quit and why don't I come the next morning and meet the guy who runs the parking lot?

"You can start work tomorrow night," Barney tells me. "It's a piece of cake. You show up at six-thirty and by midnight it's over. You work five and a half hours and people give you tips like crazy."

I think he was making fifty dollars a night doing this, which was a lot of money. This was gonna be great! Plus, during the day I could still go out and try to get gigs.

I show up the next morning; there are lots of cars in the parking lot because they're holding auditions for *Hair*.

Barney and I are standing there waiting on the parking lot guy, and he's late. All of a sudden a car pulls up. Maybe this is the guy. I'm all excited about this possible job.

Barney introduces us and the guy goes, "Hi Meat, what else do you do?" 'Cause in LA everybody does something else.

I say, "Oh, I sing." Barney tells him I'm trying to put a band together, but what I really want to do is park cars.

And this guy, Greg Carlos, looks at me and asks, "Why don't you audition for *Hair*?"

And I go, "Nah."

"You're a singer aren't you?"

"I guess."

"So audition," he says.

"Well, I'm not going to go stand in that line," I say. I haven't been able to stand in lines since my Army physical. So he takes me right on in—I'd been in the parking lot maybe seven minutes.

There was a line outside and people at the door, then once you got into the lower lobby it was full of people. Then we came to a bunch of people sitting on a flight of stairs. Then an upper lobby that's full of people, too. After that comes this inner lobby—that's absolutely crammed full of people, and finally you get into the theater. There were tables set up on the stage and people taking pictures.

I just kept following Greg Carlos until we came into the theater itself. There, on the floor of the center aisle, we found a guy completely wrapped in beads, lying on a giant pillow.

This guy Greg, whom I don't know from Adam, whispers something to the guy on the pillow who turns out to be the director, Armand Coullet. He gives me the once-over and tells me to go ahead onto the stage.

"What music did you bring?" the piano player asks me.

"I didn't bring any music. I came to get a job in the parking lot."

"You're a singer, aren't you?" the director yells from his pillow. "So sing."

Right.

"Just play the sixteen-bar blues in C," I said, "but there's this weird place, so you just have to follow me."

I began singing "The World Is Alright, It's the People that Make It Bad." I got sixteen bars out and they stopped me.

"Hold on," says Armand Coullet. "What're you doing tonight?"

"Well, I'm hoping to have the job in the parking lot. Barney's making good money out there." Everybody laughed.

"Okay, but would you like to come back tonight and watch the show?"

"I don't know." I was still worrying about that parking lot job.

"Well," says Armand, "what if I was to say to you that we would like to hire you to do the show, would you come back tonight and watch it?"

So I went back that night to watch the show, and oh, that cast was loaded. Dolores Hall was in the show, and she was as good as Aretha. *As* good.

Anyway, I never did get to see the show. I'm sitting in the audience watching and about halfway through all of a sudden this water starts coming down. And I'm applauding. Like, great effect—how're they doing that? I turn to somebody and say, "Do they do this every night?" And the guy, who up to that point hadn't been paying attention, suddenly says, "Oh my God!"

Somehow the fire sprinklers had been set off. And so I didn't get to see the show. It was closed for the next two days.

Eventually I figured out why they wanted to hire me. A big guy was leaving the cast, and here I am—another big guy. It was like equal opportunity for the larger-than-life men. I don't know whether he was really leaving or just trying to get them to give him a raise or something, because the minute they brought me in the guy said, "I don't *know* if I'm gonna leave the show."

It's just human nature I guess, but they'd already hired me and signed the Equity contract. I was supposed to start rehearsals in three days, but at some point during that period of time Big Guy #1 must have said to himself, "They think they can replace *me*? Think again!" So Armand said, "Listen to me. We're going to open up a Detroit company of *Hair*, do you know any good singers there?"

I looked at him and said, "Are you kidding? I just left there!"

"You did? Do you know any singers there?"

"I know *everybody*," I said. "I know the musicians, I know the singers, I know the best short-order cooks."

"Well, we want you to sing 'Aquarius.' We want you to do General Ulysses S. Grant. We want you to do the Young Recruit, the blah blah." Come to think of it, going back to Detroit was *just* what I wanted to do.

I loved that show. I really went out of my way to be funny. I had the look, the hair, and I did the longest General Grant in history. It's a two-minute bit basically, it comes on and it's over. One night I got timed doing it for seventeen minutes!

They were paying me base of $187.50 a week. But if you play all these other things, they said, you get paid an extra $12.50 for each one. So I would be making like $260 by the time I got to Detroit. "Plus it's an out-of-town Equity," they said, "so it automatically goes up to three hundred dollars." Wow! This was great. The only thing I wouldn't do was take my clothes off. You got an extra $12.50 a night if you stripped. I didn't want to frighten anybody, so I passed on that.

"Do you know any girls who can really sing?" they asked me.

"Well, there's one I can think of."

just a legal thing

She was in a band called the Wilson Mower Pursuit. "Her name is Stoney," I said, "and she is absolutely fantastic." They tracked her down and hired her to play Sheila, the female lead in *Hair*.

Since I was singing "Aquarius," doing a bunch of other stuff, and because of my size, I was getting more attention than anybody else. I remember getting my picture on the front page of the *Detroit Free Press* alongside a picture of Nixon. My picture was bigger! Man, I got a kick out of that. A few weeks before, I'd been parking cars. *Hoping* to park cars, actually.

I got more and more press and all of a sudden here come the offers! The first day of *Hair*, I talked to Dennis Coffey, who was a great rhythm and blues guitar player and had a label. Sugar Schwartz, some A&R guy from Atlantic, showed up. A guy from Buddah records came around. And Motown.

I ended up going to see this guy Harry Balk at Motown. He offers to sign me but asks if I want to make it a duet.

"Who with?" I want to know. "Stoney," he says. And I'm in.

Motown wanted to give us contracts, but they had this rule: They wouldn't let contracts out of the building. If you wanted to sign with Motown, you had to bring a lawyer to that building!

I didn't know any lawyers, but Stoney had a friend who knew one. So we go down to see him and at one point I asked the lawyer if they were going to go down to Motown with us.

"You don't need to go down there," he says. "I know that Motown contract. *This* is the contract that you want to sign." And he throws a contract at me.

"This is Holland, Dozier, and Holland's label," he says. *They* want to sign you." I wish I'd gone with them, but I didn't. I didn't even know who they were.

"But we were supposed to go to Motown," I'm whining. Stoney agrees and we get up to leave.

"You're making a mistake," he says. "You wanna be here."

Stoney and I go down to Motown by ourselves. The guy puts the contract down and asks, "Where's your lawyer?"

"It's a long story," I tell him. I start reading the contract. A lot of mumbo-jumbo. I read that our advance is going to be $6.25. I remember this really clearly: $6.25. I ask about it and he says, "Oh, that's just like a legal thing we have to do."

A *legal thing*? Weird comment coming from a lawyer.

"We just have to, uh, *say* we're only giving you $6.25," he tells me. "You know, *pretend*." Say, what?

"Yeah," I say, "but it says here that all you *have* to give me is $6.25 every year for seven years. I'm not going to sign this."

"Well, *I'm* signing," says Stoney. I didn't sign it. I left. Meanwhile, Stoney wants to know why.

"Kiddo, they're giving us $6.25! We need somebody to read this."

She's disgusted with me. "Eh! It's not that big of a deal."

Nightly these guys from Motown came to the show and backstage, trying to persuade us. I remember them following us out to the parking lot waving contracts. My mind was racing.

Now they're getting impatient. "We're not going to let you sit on this forever, you know." And then they throw out the bait. "We've got this song that we were going to give to the Jackson Five, but we'll give it to you guys if you'll sign. It's gonna be a monster hit."

"Hmm," I'm thinking. "The Jackson Five." I go down there to hear the song. It's called "What You See Is What You Get," and it's *great*.

"The Jacksons want to do this real bad," they say. "Don't wait too long." Reader, I signed.

Ít's either you
or the jackson five

This is how Motown worked. These guys Mike and Russ Vovano would cut a track, then call us up and have us come in and do the vocals. We'd go in, sit around, and try to learn the song. Stoney was a great singer, much better than me, and she popped that vocal off in no time flat. But it takes me a while. I'm really having trouble with it.

They're threatening us with the Jackson Five again, "If you don't get this vocal we're giving it to the Jacksons." Life at Motown was on fast forward. Everything was "*Now! Now! Now!*"

There were all these amazing people coming and going. Stevie Wonder would be in the same studio right before us. He was working on *Innervisions*. All that great stuff, I'd never heard anything like it. I'm listening through the door thinking that is *unbelievable*. Stevie actually came in and played on one of the Stoney and Meat Loaf tracks.

Bob Babbit and James Jamerson, two Motown bass players, played on our record. The Motown session guys were all over this thing—they did the horn arrangements, too. They were going to put out "What You See Is What You Get," but they didn't want anybody to know we were white.

Motown took out a full-page add in *Billboard*, which was pretty astounding. We were in silhouette and it read, "417 pounds of soul—Stoney and Meat Loaf." Stoney weighed 117 and I weighed 300. The headline was all in red and black. But they wouldn't show any pictures of us. It was then that I said to them, "Listen, let's film me and Stoney doing this," and they looked at me like I was nuts. Like why in the world would we want to do a thing like that?

Even in 1970, all I wanted was a video. I kept preaching this stuff. For years I kept saying, "Man you gotta do this" and they would say, "What's the point? You just ruin the live show."

"No, you don't," I'd say. "It's just giving them *more images.* More images is better!"

Okay, so now I'm with Motown and "What You See" gets to number eleven on the R&B charts. The producers for the Dramatics hear our song and they like it so much they decide to write their own song using the same title. They just came up with their own riff.

When R&B stations found out we were white—I wonder how that happened—we were dropped like a stone, and the Dramatics came on and had a number one record.

Then we recorded "Who Is the Leader of the People?" It was a great song. Sounded like one of those Temptations things, and it was rockin'. But Motown said they didn't want Stoney and Meat Loaf putting out this song.

They wanted Edwin Starr—he'd just had a big hit with "War!" They wanted this to go to him. So he releases it, and on the track you hear my and Stoney's vocals, all the background parts. They just took our lead off and stuck his on.

I went in and demanded to see Berry Gordy, the head of Motown. Went into this boardroom full of people. I wanted to be very dramatic about this whole thing and tell him I thought it was bullshit, so I took my shoe off and banged it on the desk. Like Khrushchev. But nothing changed, except that we never recorded for them again.

𝔄pples! bananas!

Meanwhile, we were still doing *Hair* in Detroit, and working with a local Detroit band called Jake Wade and the Soul Searchers. They were all black, except for Stoney's boyfriend, the lead guitar player. They played backup for Aretha Franklin and other black stars when they came to town.

Jake Wade was so funny. He aspired to have a pimp style and wore one of those *Shaft* hats. He was straight out of a seventies blaxploitation movie. He spoke to you like a record playing at slow speed. *Muauw muauw muauw.* I couldn't understand a word he said.

There was a flute player in the band named Aaron, who was

very intelligent. He was a brilliant flute player, and he would interpret Jake for me.

"Jake says that if we're going to go do this, we're going to have to get a raise for the band." And Jake would mumble some more, whisper something, and I'd ask Aaron to translate. "Well, Jake says . . ."

We opened for Red Rock—Ricky Cobb, whom I'd grown up with, was the drummer. It was our first show with Jake Wade and the Soul Searchers. So we're all back there, and I'm saying, "What do we do if we get an encore?"

"You don't get no encore."

"Don't be saying that, what're we going to do?"

"I don't know," they said. "We only do thirty-five minutes' worth of music and that's it."

"If we get an encore," I said, "you just go out and start playing something that Stoney knows how to sing, and get into 'What You See' again."

They knew Stoney could sing but they didn't think that I was too hot. And they were right. Compared to Stoney, no. Compared to Aretha Franklin and all the other people they backed up, no. But I looked at them and I said, "Let me tell you something, guys. Do not be surprised by *anything* I do." They had no idea what was about to happen.

Well, we got out there and did the show in the Buffalo Auditorium. The audience went wild. They called for an encore and wouldn't stop.

We went out and knocked 'em dead. Stoney was ripping and I was yelling and screaming, and then, when we'd got them going, I jumped off the stage and got into the middle of the audience with a mike, as far as I could get. I got these people completely nuts. I got 'em quiet, then I got 'em to jump up and down. I got 'em to sit on the floor. I got 'em to start yelling "apples," I got 'em to start yelling "bananas." I was like a little Hitler. Fun.

Stoney's singing and I'm rockin' and running from side to side and doing all this stuff and I turn around and it's all over. People are going crazy. We came offstage and these guys just *looked* at me, like "What happened?"

"Stick around," I said.

how do i look in my pimpmobile?

I don't know how many shows we actually played with Jake Wade and the Soul Searchers, but it was a lot. We played in Baltimore, we played in Buffalo; did a gig with Richie Havens at the New Haven Coliseum. We had a gig in Detroit opening for Sly and the Family Stone. That got canceled, which was a big drag, 'cause Sly never showed up. Anywhere.

And then we went down South as the opening act for Rare Earth, which was an interesting experience because of Jake Wade. We were just a rock-and-roll band except for Jake. He affected this pimp drop-dead cool look. By the time we were headed South I knew he was kinda accepting me because he let me sit up front with him in the pimpmobile, this tricked-out Cadillac he had. But if I was going to ride with him in the front seat, I couldn't just sit there like some uptight honky passenger. I had to get into the Jake Wade groove.

The way he would drive is with one hand on the wheel and his elbow resting on the seat so his hand would touch the brim of his pimp hat. So laid back it looked as if he might just fall asleep. He'd lean way into the right and if I was to keep up the vibe I had to lean way into him on the left. Two coolfry bookends.

Jake had taken the roof off his Cadillac and replaced it with a Lucite dome, so there was this green plastic bubble up there on top of the car. We took this outlandish vehicle down South and it wasn't well received. Whenever we'd pull into a motel, we'd get dirty looks. They'd refuse to allow the black members of the band to *enter* the place, never mind stay there. And this was in the seventies! They wouldn't let Jake eat in the restaurant. Their attitude was like, "Are you guys out of your minds? You can't bring a black person in here." They refused to serve him. We'd go in these restaurants, and just sit there forever.

And that pimpmobile! You've never seen such looks from both black *and* white. I mean, we were crossing the Mississippi once, and I remember riding in this Cadillac past all these tiny little shacks along the side of the road, little shotgun shacks—the kind of shanties in which you see desperately poor blacks living in *South Africa*. It wasn't

that far removed from the road between Johannesburg and Sun City. And when that Cadillac came by, it was like some spaceship had landed in their backyard. People would come running out of their houses. "Whoa! Baby, you gotta see this crazy thing!"

We didn't play that many gigs, maybe fifteen, but we stormed. That was one cooking live band. Stoney was so great, and combined with Jake Wade's funky chops and my crazy theatrical antics, it was like this wild element that just blew into town. Eventually Rare Earth didn't want us to open for them anymore. Who would?

Íf í had a gun ín my hand í would shoot you

I'd just got back from the Jake Wade and the Soul Searchers tour when I got a call from Armand Coullet. He said, "We're putting together an all-star cast of *Hair* on Broadway. We'd like you to sing 'Aquarius.'" They fired a bunch of people from the New York cast and brought in eleven or twelve people from Los Angeles—and me from Detroit.

I'd never been to New York before. As soon as I land at the airport, I'm freaked out. Every twenty seconds, I'm going, "Wow, man!" They put me in this hotel, a one-bedroom kind of deal. When I opened the closet there was this huge hole in the back. It was like, "Oh Gosh! Rats are gonna come in here!"

Now, when you join a troupe of *Hair*, they give you these yellow and red beads in a leather bag and they tell you, "These beads were strung at an Indian reservation. They're real Indian beads, and they have real spiritual power, so wear 'em and feel the mystic vibe, you know?" Everybody wore the beads all the time. The different companies of *Hair* were called tribes. If we went to Toronto, all the *Hair* people there had their beads. Went to Chicago once. All the *Hair* people had their beads on, too.

When I got to New York, the producers told me to report to the office. I go in, they tell me, "Go to the back, they're waiting for you." On my way, I pass by two secretaries, and on their desk is a stack of little leather pouches and boxes of beads. These two New York secretaries sitting in this office stringing the *Hair* beads. And I went, "Ah man! Hook, line, and sinker!"

I signed the contract, and they said, "Okay, you're only gonna rehearse two or three days, because you know the show. It's the same dances, same thing, it's just a matter of getting to know the cast." Half the cast had been fired, of course, but I didn't think about what the repercussions of this might be.

The first night we're going on, I walk over and sign in a half-hour early. I go up the stairs and say, "Hi, how you doing?" as I pass

by this black girl. She looks at me and goes, "Don't say 'hi' to me. Don't say shit to me, motherfucker. You came in here, you replaced my good friend. Let me tell you something, if I had a gun in my hand I would shoot you."

"Oh!" I think, "this isn't going to be all that much fun."

Remember this is *Hair*, and *Hair* is the peace and love musical, right? Well, the long and short of it is, between the hostility and another concussion, I didn't last long in New York. One of the rigging pipes broke and swung down and hit me smack in the head. I went out like a light. It knocked me out, knocked me off the stage as a matter of fact. Concussion number fifteen. Lucky it didn't kill me.

After that, I broke out in a stress-related rash. My skin looked like I had third-degree burns. I had to go to a clinic and sit in a tub of cortisone. It got so bad I asked to be sent to another company of *Hair*, told them I couldn't handle New York City anymore. So they sent me to...Pittsburgh! That was the big joke for a while. You went from Broadway to Pittsburgh? Smart move, Meat.

Go for the maniac

Eventually I wound up doing *Hair* in Buffalo, where I ran into a couple of actors who were doing *Grease* on Broadway. They told me that the actor who sings "Greased Lightning" in *Grease* was leaving and that I would be perfect for the part. I applied for the role and they were going to hire me, but on my way to the theater to sign contracts, I ran into Jim Rado, one of the writers of *Hair*. When I told him where I was going, he said, "You don't want to do that, you want to come do my play." When I told the people in *Grease* I wasn't doing the part because I had just run into Jim Rado on the street, naturally they weren't too happy. I learned not to do *that* too often.

Jim Rado's new play was *Rainbow*. It was the follow-up to *Hair*. The adventures of Claude in Rainbowland.

Jeff Hunter was Raul Julia's agent at the time, and when I finally found out what it is an agent does, he became mine, too. The first thing he did was to send me to the Public Theater to audition for *More Than You Deserve*. And that's where I first met Jim Steinman. I sang "I'd Love to Be as Heavy as Jesus," and Steinman was the only one in this room. He was a slightly unnerving presence. Long black hair, ornate black leather jacket. Kind of glowering at me.

Now that I know Steinman really well, I know why he was the only one in the room. He doesn't like anyone to violate his space. After I'd sung, he told me, "Wait here."

I sat in this room waiting and waiting. I'm saying to myself, "This is a stupid waste of time." I was just about ready to leave when, half an hour later, in comes this army: Joe Papp and seven other people. They all sat down and stared at me. Finally, Jim says, "Sing that song again." I sing the song again, but they stop me before I finish. "Listen, we'd really like for you to do this play," says Joe Papp. It was a Michael Weller play. And I said, "Oh, okay!"

This is the first time anybody had ever handed me a script. On a piece of paper inside the script, they listed four different characters. Joe said, "Take the script, read it, and we want to see you back here on Monday. You tell me which character you want to play."

The next day, I read the script. "Now what?" I thought. I was mildly panicked, so I called Armand Coullet. He was living in New York with his wife, Rhonda, downtown in the Village. I figured he'd know what to do. He graduated from the University of Mississippi as valedictorian, and his major was Latin! He was a mad genius type, God rest his soul.

"Did you read the script?" he asked.

"Uh huh."

"When you were reading it, did you get bored with it and put it down?"

"Nope, I found it funny in a horrible way."

"Who wrote it?"

"Michael Weller."

"He's good. Did it offend you?"

"Yup."

"That's good. Black comedy?"

"Yup."

I told him about having to choose among the four characters.

"Which one do you personally find the most interesting?"

"Well, there's this character called Rabbit who's a junkie, who goes around and blows people up with grenades. Not the enemy, but his own people. 'Cause he's nuts, he's crazy. He thinks that he's sending them *home*. He thinks he's really a nice guy. He really *is* a nice guy, but he's just gone completely over the top."

"That's the spirit," says Armand. "Go for the maniac!"

Armand thought it was perfect that I wanted to play a three-hundred-pound junkie who blows up his fellow soldiers.

I went back to see Joe on Monday. "Which character did you prefer?" they wanted to know. Rabbit. They looked at me a little funny. "You *did* read the script, didn't you? Well okay, Rabbit you are."

We did it as a workshop. In that play were Kathleen Widdoes and Steve Collins. Eventually Ron Silver did it, too, and Fred Gwynne. All these great actors. Mary Beth Hurt played a little old Oriental man. She was unbelievable. Dolores Hall even wound up in this play eventually.

So that was my character. A goodhearted maniac who wants to help out by blowing people up. A little touch of typecasting. Whenever he hears a soldier complaining, "God I wish I could be home!" he goes, "Ummm, well, okay." And just blows him up.

When my character gets a letter from home, it becomes apparent that not only is he nuts, his whole family is crazy. He gets this really funny letter that goes, "Dear Rabbit, Things are okay here. The big news last week was your no-account brother got up to his mischief again, and went in and shot that good pastor Manderville and a portion of the congregation to smithereens with a shotgun that Daddy bought him for Christmas. Sheriff came and took him back to jail, but Billy promised he would never do it again, so sheriff let him go. Okay, that's all except, oh yeah, the big news was your wife ran off with that Frank feller, but don't pay it no mind, 'cause she weren't no good anyhow. Your lovin' Maw."

Then I'd go into this song called "More Than You Deserve." The hook of the song is in the last verse, which goes: "Then I saw you making love to two of my friends/ so I looked them right in their eyes and said, 'Listen up/ why don't you take some more, boys? It's more than you deserve.'"

It was such a wild lyric that when I sang it on opening night it stopped the show! There was a standing ovation. I was in an absolute state of shock. The next night, the same thing happened. I began to get really nervous—like, "Am I expected to deliver this every night?"

meat loaf TO HELL AND BACK

As you like it

After the show closed, Papp wanted to do it again at Lincoln Center. "Hell no," I said. I was being honest, and by this time I was in a show at La Mama. But he put Mary Beth Hurt and me on salary anyway—whether we worked or not. He put me in a few Shakespeare plays. I did *As You Like It*, with Raul and Mary Beth. David Rabe was the director.

When I went to read for *As You Like It*, Rabe looked at me and said, "That's the worst Shakespeare I have ever heard in my entire life." Shakespeare with a Texas accent is not a pretty thing. I'd just come back from a trip to Texas and I still had a thick Southern accent that did not go too well with Shakespearean English.

Rabe was about to give me the lethal "Thank you" when Papp leaned over and whispered something in his ear. "Meat," he said, "here's a copy of *As You Like It*." Again, they had this piece of paper with four characters written on it. "Go home and read this, then come back and tell me which character you want to play." I went home. I was in a quandary again.

Shakespeare's really tough. I'm reading it and I can't make neither head nor tail of it. I'm wondering what in the world is going on. Fate, as in so many of Shakespeare's plays, intervened—this time in the form of *TV Guide*. On channel 9 in New York, they used to have a show called the *Million Dollar Movie*. Well, that particular night, it was Mickey Rooney in *A Midsummer Night's Dream*.

"Aah! Well, I should take a look at this," I thought. I start watching and I'm going, "Ooohh, this is interesting!" because they're not barding it up. All they're doing is sitting around talking. They're in the woods, a bunch of them sitting around this campfire, and they're speaking like you and I might speak. So when I start reading the play, I'm trying *not* to think of the words the way you usually think of Shakespeare being performed—declaiming the lines.

I picked Amiens as my character in *As You Like It*. The one with the most dialogue, the biggest part of the four I was offered. I'm sure they thought that, given my reading, I would go for the fewest possible lines. But whatever part I chose, I knew I was going to get to sing the song "Blow, Blow Thou Winter Wind."

These actors were very serious. Even doing a Shakespearean

comedy, they were serious. And they thought I was crazy. There were fake trees, and being a born ham, I couldn't resist hiding behind them. Or I'd say, "More of this anon," and I'd run to another tree and finish my lines. Joe Papp was yelling, "Meat Loaf!!! Will you cut that out!!!"

On opening night, all the critics were there. I was singing "Blow, Blow Thou Winter Wind," and Clive Barnes, the critic for the *New York Times*, was fast asleep in the front row, which was on the same level as the stage. I was within four or five feet of him when I got to the end of the song. I purposely ended on a really loud note and woke him up. He jumped out of his seat—it scared him out of his wits—but he gave us a good review anyway.

The next night I'm late for the theater. I run off the bus in such a mad frenzy that I forget there are *stairs*, going down. So I just run straight off the top step and smash my head on the top of the door. I slip down the stairs, *bam! bam! bam!* I'm sitting in the gutter on Eighty-sixth Street when the bus pulls away, almost running me over. Concussion number sixteen. And counting.

I get to the play just in time to go on, but for the life of me I can't remember my first line. My scene is crucial because it introduces Jacques famous speech, "All the world's a stage and all the men and women merely players." I'm so out of it, I come out with a line that's a page and a half into the scene.

Fred Coffin, who was playing Jacques, looks at me, stunned. "Dost thou know what thou speakest?" he asks in mock Shakespearean. I'm thinking to myself, "What is this moron talking about??" So I respond, "Thou talkest passing strange, sire."

Fred comes back, "You are an errant knave to talk such poncey rubbish."

We're adlibbing Shakespeare for quite awhile before I come to my senses and bring the scene around to the beginning. As we leave the stage Fred says, "Thoust were indeed a naughty varmit" or some stupid thing, and we're both cracking up.

In the fall, Joe Papp brought *More Than You Deserve* back. The first performance was truly deadly. It was as if they really had brought in dead people from that big cemetery out in Queens. Dug them up and brought them in—it was a matinee full of blue-haired ladies they'd bused in from somewhere, and who had no business at a black comedy about junkies, blowing people up, and gang rape.

The female lead gets gang-raped by a bunch of soldiers and really loves it—sings a *song* about how she loves it. The play starts off in a hospital, everybody wrapped in bandages, hooked up to IV drips. Suddenly all the patients in the beds burst into song. There's about fifteen of us, dancing around and swinging the IV bottles. A very sick play. These old ladies were not its target audience.

I had a scene with Fred Gwynne; he was playing the commanding officer who comes on complaining about wanting to go home. Naturally, my character starts planning to *send* him home. This particular matinee, Fred comes out, says the first line of the scene, and then goes to the last line and walks off the stage. What the hell is going on? I scramble around as best I can saying this line and that line. I was absolutely beside myself. The stage manager sees murder in my eyes and he grabs me, "Meat, calm down. We've got to finish the play." I'm trying not to scream. We finish the play and I go down to the dressing room and I pick Fred up by his shirt—he's a big guy—pin him up against the locker, and start screaming at him at the top of my lungs. "How dare you?"

"I'm going to bring you up on charges!" he says.

Here comes Joe Papp downstairs. "Meat, what are you doing?" Joe calmed us down, made us apologize to each other. "Meat, you apologize," he said.

"Fred, look," I said. "I'm really sorry. That was really over the top."

He could tell I was sincere. And, with his big mournful face, he said, "I'm sorry, too. I've never done anything like that before. It was just this audience, I lost my mind. I just went crazy."

Besides my character, there was another maniac involved in the production: Jim Steinman. *More Than You Deserve* began as a play with a bit of music in it. One or two songs in both acts. Jim talked Michael Weller into turning it into a full-blown musical. It's not that the music wasn't any good, but Jim was trying to make it into something bigger than it was. They tried to make this weird black comedy into a big Broadway musical. The first time we'd performed it, we did it with some wooden boxes and a table and an upright piano. Then they brought in all these people, black gospel singers, dancers, a choreographer. It was insane. They put snow flock on the Christmas tree, and you know how tacky *that* is. Then they hung red balls on it—and strings of popcorn. They totally ruined the play.

Jim was in his most flamboyant period. The gloves and the

cape. That all came from this Wagnerian show he wrote, *Das Rheingold*. He would come out in these crazy outfits and weird make-up and pound the piano and do stuff that was totally out there. *Das Rheingold* was hysterical—and bizarre. It had some pretty good people in it. Richard Gere was in it—that's how Richard and I met.

When I sang the title song in this last production of *More Than You Deserve* people were yelling, "Encore" after my song in the middle of the first act, and it interrupted the show. In order to deal with this, they had to write a reprise into the scene with the soldiers saying "Wow! Will you sing that chorus again?" It was stupid. Still, I've never seen anything like it in the theater. Ever! It went on every night, and I got nominated for an Obie. Everybody wanted me to be in everything after that, and soon I became a spoiled little brat.

Jeff, my agent, would call up and go, "Meat, they'd like for you to come down and audition." I'd say, "Nah. I don't feel like doing that." Or I'd go down and I'd sing a song and I'd leave. And then he'd call me back and say, "They want you to come back in." And I'd say, "No. They've seen me. They know what I can do. They want me, they can hire me."

I was so full of myself and I hadn't even made it yet. It would get worse before it got better.

Steinman and me

During my theater days in New York, I lead a schizophrenic existence. I'd get out of my tights and doublet at the theater, put on my leather jacket, and head to Max's Kansas City where I'd jam with local bands far into the night. My specialties were R&B classics "Barefootin'" and "In the Midnight Hour." It was a world away from Shakespeare.

I'm also trying to talk Jim Steinman into doing an album with me, but Jimmy wants Kim Milford as his lead singer. Kim Milford was tall, skinny, and good-looking, with long blond hair. He looked like a rock star, and I, well, didn't.

I hassled Jim and hassled him and hassled him. I went over to see Robert Stigwood, head of RSO Records, to make my case. Stigwood had seen me perform and he told Jim, "No, no, no! Forget Milford. Meat Loaf's the guy. This is the guy I want to sign."

So Jim was dragged kicking and screaming into the future. We signed to RSO Records and cut "More Than You Deserve," as a single. On the B side, I did that George Harrison song, "In the Presence of the Lord." They pressed the radio copies of the single and started sending them up to Boston. The Boston guys loved it and the big station in Boston was playing it up to twelve times a day at one point, which is enormous exposure.

The day that the retail copies are supposed to come out, I go to Stigwood's office—which is just around the corner from my apartment. There is a receptionist sitting there whom I have never seen before.

"Hi. I'm—" I start to say when I look down and see all these boxes of 45s. My records. Boxes and boxes and boxes and boxes of them stacked in the lobby.

"Oh, great!" I say. "Can I have one?"

"Absolutely not."

"But that's my record."

"I'm sorry."

"Is Johnny Bienstock in?"

"Mr. Bienstock no longer works here."

"Well, he was here the day before yesterday."

"I'm sorry, sir. He is no longer employed here."

I drop a few more names. And for each person I name, she comes back with the same robotic response: "I'm sorry sir, he's no longer with the company."

"You know what?" I say. "Screw you!"

And with that I walked right in. Unfortunately, there was nobody in the offices. *Any* of the offices. It looked like someone had dropped the neutron bomb. Robert Stigwood had gotten rid of the entire staff of RSO Records—the day my record came out.

I came back out and the cyborg secretary says, "Sir, if you don't vacate the premises immediately, I'm going to have to call security."

"Call away," I say, "but those are my records and I'm taking them." I picked up three 45s and walked out. *Three copies*—that's all I've ever seen of it. I don't know what ever happened to all those boxes. "More Than You Deserve" never got any further than that station in Boston.

improvisation

Sometime in 1972, I was walking from my apartment on Seventy-fourth Street up to the Delacorte Theater, where I was doing Shakespeare in the Park. I passed by these three Spanish guys right across from the Metropolitan Museum. They looked at me and they were like laughing at my size. They crept up behind me but I ignored them. Then they started poking me. They were saying things in Spanish, like "Hey, fat guy." Real original. I didn't say a word.

They kept at it, pushing me and poking at me. I stopped in my tracks, turned around, put my arms out wide like King Kong, and ran at them full speed, screaming at the top of my lungs. I scared the wits out of them. There were five or six black guys across the street waiting for a bus by the museum—they applauded. The fear didn't take me until it was over.

The only other time that I ever got bothered in New York was when Jim and I were walking down the street having this really bizarre conversation. It was about ten-thirty at night. We were at Lincoln Center, Sixty-seventh Street, walking up Columbus Avenue, when a guy says to me, "Give me your wallet, I've got a gun."

And I turned to him and I said, "Come on. I ain't got time for this now, okay?" We kept walking.

The guy didn't move. We got down almost to the end of the block and I turned to Jim and I said, "What did that guy just say? Did that guy say, 'Give me your wallet'?"

And Jim answers, "What guy?" We turned around and looked back at this guy and he was just standing back there screaming at us, because we'd ignored him. We didn't run, didn't cuss him out, didn't give him the wallet either. Our reaction wasn't in the script, which infuriated him. Nobody ever taught him how to improvise.

the piano just keeled over and died, ma'am

One time, Jim and I were rehearsing "For Crying Out Loud." It was a song he'd written before I met him, and Andre DeShields, who's also an actor, had done it previously over at the Manhattan Theater Club. He's really good, but I've always thought that nobody can sing a Jim Steinman song like I can. I told that to Jimmy when we first started working together and he wouldn't have it. "Oh no, no. Please. I'm the only one who really knows how to sing them. I *wrote* them." Eventually Jimmy's mother told him, "You know what? Meat Loaf knows you better than anybody. He knows you better than I do."

Anyway, Jim and I were working over in the Ansonia Hotel, home of the Continental Baths. Bette Midler got her start playing there. They had small rehearsal rooms you could rent, just big enough for a piano. We spent a lot of time there, four or five hours a day. We were rehearsing "Crying Out Loud," and right while I'm singing, he stops me and he goes, "Listen. Andre did this thing when he sang it—"

And I said, "Don't you *ever* mention another singer's name while I'm singing! I don't give a shit what Andre DeShields did. I know what I'm doing, and what Andre did is what Andre did. He doesn't know how to sing this the way I do, and neither do you!"

Jim still wanted to make his point. "But I'm just trying to tell you..." And I got—this is my uncontrollable temper—*really furious*, and I picked up the piano and turned it over on its side, CRASH! It was an old, rickety piano, and when I tipped it over the pedals just stayed there on the floor, right where they'd been.

Jimmy is sitting on the bench. He's never left the bench. He's not reacting. While he's staring dumbfounded at the pedals that've come off, they keel over as well. Now I realize what I've done, and I don't even know how I did it. Here's this piano sitting on its side and Jim doesn't say a word. A few moments go by and then he smiles and says, "I guess you're right." He's not going to argue with an over-turned piano.

But I'm panicked, "Oh my God. What did I do? What did I do? What've I done?" When I get mad, two minutes later, I'm over it. I'm thinking, "Oh, I'm sorry... I shouldn't have done that. Oh, my heavens. Oh, man, I'm so stupid! I can't believe it."

I put the piano upright, and I'm sitting and trying to put these pedals back up and they just keep falling out. I'm going, "What am I going to do now?" Then I think, "Gum!" I've always chewed gum when I sing, so, I have all this gum. I take a big wad and start chewing it, and then I put all this chewed gum on the top of the pedals and stick them up there and, to my amazement, they stay!

"Let's get out of here," I tell Jim, and we do. Fast. I'm sure somebody went in there that afternoon, put his foot on the pedal, and it fell right off.

When we came back the next day, we asked the lady at the desk, "Have you got a different room for us today? We didn't care for the timbre on that piano."

Meat loaf is in the details

Sam Ellis eventually became the first mate on the deranged maiden voyage of the S.S. *Bat Out of Hell* when it finally set sail in 1977. Sam came into my life a few years earlier when I did *Rainbow* again in Washington, D.C. I'd already been in the off-Broadway production, and now they'd revamped it and taken it down to the Kennedy Center in D.C. And at this point they called me up and said, "Look, the guy we got down here to do this is not working out, could you come down and replace him? We're just gonna do a little two- or three-week run. What do you think?" And I said okay. Sam Ellis was the stage manager, and he met me at the theater. Must have been sometime in the winter of '73.

Now, whenever I do theater, I inevitably get made Equity deputy because I know the union regulation book backwards and I'm not afraid to call the producer on the tiniest infraction. If it's the designated time for a break: "Oops! we'll have to stop here. We get the ten-minute break now! You're running over, if we go past this fifteen minutes you owe everybody money!" I got a reputation as I went from show to show; I did it at Shakespeare in the Park. Meat Loaf, Equity deputy.

So when I went to do *Rainbow* off-Broadway, because of my reputation for being such a pain in the neck, they offered me more money *not* to be Equity deputy. And I said no. My reputation! I was so into this stuff, the minutiae. When I got to the theater, the first thing I did was to go out and buy a tape measure and measure the dressing rooms. I used to be so wacky about the rule book. You're supposed to have a certain amount of space per person. Measuring height, width, length.

"Hmm, this doesn't seem right," I'd say with great authority. I could always tell when something was not up to code. I could smell it. We all got down on the floor and measured and sure enough—several inches off! They had to build the thing bigger and put different lights up and make the dressing room completely to scale. Well, the second night I was in Washington I get this phone call from Sam Ellis.

"Meat, I've got bad news," he said. "We're not going to do this show past the first week. The guy who was producing it ran out of money."

But fate was on my side. The cast came to me, wringing their hands and said, "What do we do?"

"Don't panic," I said. "Listen, it's all going to be fine. *Better*, in fact, because they've got a bond at Equity. Everybody will get paid, and not only that, you will get paid for the entire run you were *supposed* to do. You may even make more money out of it than if you'd *done* it, because there's a penalty clause. Yeah, we can cry penalty!" I'd only done the show for two days; I got paid for a month.

This apparent disaster turned out to be even more fortunate for me than just some extra money. I went home, and no sooner had I walked in the door of my apartment on Seventy-fourth Street than the phone rang. Just like in the movies. I had literally set down my two little bags and was about to go down and check my mail when a guy named Brian Avnet called—he went on to manage Manhattan Transfer and now runs David Foster's record company.

"Is this Meat Loaf?"

"Speaking," I said.

He said, "We're putting on this play called the *Rocky Horror Show*. Would you be interested?"

"Yeah sure," I said. I loved the name.

"When can you come to LA?"

I said, "In about ten minutes!"

He laughed.

"Really," I said, "I'm packed."

So, you see, if the guy hadn't run out of money, I'd never have done *Rocky Horror*. I'd have been in D.C. doing that dopey show.

but where is dr. frankenfurter?

I went out West to start work on the *Rocky Horror Show.* When we got there there was no script. They just told me that *Rocky Horror* was going to be science-fiction musical comedy. Okay, cool. The first two weeks all we're doing is rehearsing music and learning songs. Still no script. Eventually we move from this little room where we've been working to a little theater and they start to bring in the script—bit by bit.

At the beginning of the play, you would walk around with these masks and funny suits on, interacting with the audience. You couldn't speak to them, but you could perform little stunts with them—like going through someone's purse or drinking their drink. After this nonverbal interaction with the audience, Jamie Lee Donnaly came out and sang "Science Fiction."

The cast is working on the show one scene at a time. My characters—Eddie and Dr. Scott—don't come in for a long time. So I have yet to do my scene with Tim Curry as Dr. Frankenfurter.

We're finally ready to rehearse Curry's entrance but we still haven't seen him. Where is the good doctor? The cast is on stage and the music starts. Doors in the back of this little theater open up and a guy with big black hair and a leather jacket comes walking down the aisle singing "Sweet Transvestite." As he gets closer we see that he's got a garter belt, fishnet stockings, and enough makeup for a cosmetics counter. And he's singing this song that none of us has ever heard before.

I'm sitting next to Graham Jarvis, the show's narrator. I turn to

meat loaf TO HELL AND BACK

him and say, "I'm leaving!" I walk across the street against the light and get a ticket for jaywalking. Graham followed me out and I asked, "What is this? What's going on? These people are nuts. I'm not doing a drag show." I didn't want to go back, but Graham's an older actor and he said you can't just walk out like that. So we went back.

Everyone saw me leave and it caused great disruption. So when I got back I'm talking to Brian Avnet and a stage manager. I'm saying, "Listen guys. I can't do this drag part. I'd feel silly."

They're telling me it's not drag. "Read the script and see what's going on here. Just trust us."

"Okay, but no way am I doing drag."

Cut to: me in fishnet stockings. Which stopped the show. Sometimes even Curry would start laughing. The whole cast would break character. Some nights I'm laughing, too. And guess what? I'm doing drag.

In the nude with raquel welch

I played two characters in *Rocky Horror*: Dr. Scott and Eddie. Eddie was a grocery delivery boy and Frankenfurter needed a brain for Rocky. So he took half of Eddie's brain because he needed only a half a brain for Rocky. They put Eddie in an icebox in case Frankenfurter needed parts later—so he's still alive in there. In the movie, Eddie came out of this freezer on a motorcycle, but in the play, Rocky was born on top of a Coca-Cola icebox that contains Eddie's body. When Rocky's born on top of this Coca-Cola freezer deal, all the heat from his birth causes Eddie to thaw out. Eddie comes out of this box singing "Whatever Happened to Saturday Night." I didn't think it made any sense, but it's a musical, what can I tell you?

They put me in the Coke box, and they put Rocky on top, and I freaked out. I started screaming and carrying on—'cause it was like that ball box I'd been locked in at my elementary school. So they cut a hole in the side right by my head. In rehearsals, it was fine. But then it came time for a dress rehearsal and the next thing you know, there's a big pipe, a big tube with dry ice coming in there. I freaked out again. Eventually, they had a Plexiglas back put on it so I could see through. Which calmed me down, somewhat.

Every rock-and-roller in town came to see the *Rocky Horror Show*. You had John Lennon coming down, Harry Nilsson coming down, you had Ringo. Sometimes they'd come backstage. Keith Moon came a lot. If he was in the house you knew it, because there were nine bottles of champagne lined up in front of the stage. Nine bottles for nine people in the cast.

One night Elvis came to see the show. He sent people over because he wanted to meet Tim Curry and me. Tim went in and saw him and I went in, but as soon as I was in the room with him I became speechless. Elvis had a gun in his belt. I just stood there like a dummy when Elvis said, "You did a real good job, son."

All I could do was spit out "Thanks." I just stood there looking at him.

He dismissed me with "Nice talking to you, son." I had the opportunity of a lifetime and I just stood there like an idiot. Later when I told this story to Lisa Marie she just laughed. I mentioned the gun. She said, "Daddy always wore guns." Like she was saying, "Daddy always wore argyles."

Famous people were always coming around. Like Charlton Heston. We would all ask, "Where is he?" In Tim's dressing room, probably. Then everyone would leave their dressing room doors open—just to watch when the star in question came out. One time Raquel Welch came and she was going up to Curry's room. My door was open, and I'm standing there stark naked. There was my door and this little hallway and there's Curry's door. Curry's door was closed, and she knocked on it and just turned around. I'm standing there naked, and my only comment was: "Oh, it's Jane Fonda!" You've never seen anybody get so mad in such a hurry in all your life. She was just horrified. I'm not sure if it was my mistaking her for someone else or my being naked. Luckily, Curry's door opened and saved us both. I wrote to her apologizing, I'm not sure what for (my naked body?). She never wrote back.

I remember the night the cast of the *Brady Bunch* came. Everybody was cracking up. We'd always know when famous people were in the audience because they would get comps. Someone would tell us Chicago Transit Authority is in the house tonight or the Stones are here tonight. I was shy—the same as I'd been with Elvis.

One time I had a meeting in Manhattan and I was early. There was a little coffee shop attached to the building, so I went in and I sat down at the counter. There was an empty stool next to me and someone sitting on the next stool. I order a coffee. There's a little sugar thing right in front of me, but I want Sweet'n Low. I glance over and see Sweet'n Low packets in front of the guy on the other stool. I didn't even look at him, I just said, "Excuse me, can you hand me the Sweet'n Low?" He answers, "Yeah, sure, mate," and he's got an English accent. Sounds familiar. I open the packet and I take a quick look and it's John Lennon. Thousands and thousands of questions are in my head. We're both Libras, close to the same birthday—I even used to *dream* about John Lennon.

I used to have dreams of going to Lennon's office, and of being signed to Apple Records by him. We would sit and talk about

music. He would be behind a desk wearing a white suit. After he died I kept having the same dream, only I could never see his face.

Anyway, I sat next to Lennon in that coffee shop for fifteen minutes and never got up the nerve to speak. I wanted to tell him I'd had the dream; I wanted to say, "I've always dreamed about coming to your office, and you were wearing white."

The two people I most idolized in the world—Elvis and Lennon—and I couldn't say a thing. I get starstruck around people, what can I tell you?

an rko production

Everybody knew they were gonna do a movie of the *Rocky Horror Show,* and we were all wondering if we were gonna have a part in it. Kim Milford kept walking around saying "I'm playing Rocky in the movie." So they called this meeting before the show one night. A couple of days before, they had come to me and said, "We want you to play Eddie in the movie." I asked about Dr. Scott, but they had decided to separate the parts. I said, "Okay, but that's a mistake." And they said, "Be happy you're playing Eddie." I said I was. And then they told me not to tell anybody.

At the cast meeting they told Richard O'Brien, the creator, that he was gonna play Riff Raff. Two people from London, Pat Quinn who played Magenta and Little Nell who played Columbia, were going to be in the movie. And Tim was obviously going to play Frankenfurter. They said they were hiring two American actors, Susan Sarandon and Barry Bostwick, to play Brad and Janet. And I was going to play Eddie. They hired a German bodybuilder to play Rocky. Graham Jarvis was hoping to get the part of the narrator, but they'd hired a guy who'd been in James Bond movies, an English guy.

While we were still doing *Rocky Horror* in LA, Lou Adler liked to play basketball. He put up a rim in the parking lot between the Rainbow and the Roxy. Me and Lou went down there with Avnet and different people and the parking lot guys. One day in '72 or '73, Lou brought this guy with him that I knew from somewhere.

I'm playing with Avnet and he says you guard this guy. I recognize him, but I can't think of his name. I ask Avnet, "This guy that I'm guarding, what's his name?"

"That's Jack Nicholson!" So I'm guarding Jack Nicholson in this parking lot in the afternoon, playing basketball. Avnet says to me, "Adler can't hit from the right side and Nicholson can't hit from the left. So I'll keep Adler on the right side and you keep Nicholson on the left side, right?" At one point I'm guarding Nicholson and I say, "Hey, if I let you make the shot will you put me in your next movie?" "Yeah, kid," he says, "of course." So I move and the shot goes *swish!*

"So am I in your next movie?"

shakespeare, et al.

"Nope."

"But you said—"

"Don't believe everything you hear, kid," he tells me. Good advice, and I'd need it later on.

In the movie, they had a stunt double riding the motorcycle that Eddie rides in on. When I was on the bike, it wasn't even running. The stunt double crashed through the big ice wall and then they cut to a close-up of me. All I had to do was coast to a stop. In one part, the motorcycle in the movie is running down the ramp. They had to figure out how they could get close-ups of me up on that ramp.

They took the windshield and handlebars off the motorcycle and put me in a wheelchair and rolled me across the top.

Then the plan changed. "What we'll do is have you come down the ramp. You all right coming down the ramp?"

I said, "Yeah. I don't see why not."

So I made this little trial run down the ramp and stopped before I got to the end. They tried to shoot the scene by putting the camera at the bottom of the ramp, but that didn't work. So they mounted the camera to the front of the wheelchair. So you can see the handlebars and the round visor.

That made it so top-heavy that when you got down to the bottom of the ramp, you didn't just kind of coast off like you did before. Now when I went down the ramp the wheelchair hit the edge, flipped over, and smashed the camera. My stand-in (not my stunt double) leaped forward to try to catch me and the wheelchair. He caught his leg on the side of the ramp.

So the camera smashed, I think I got a little cut, and the guy broke his leg. Everyone's trying to help me while my stand-in's over there, screaming in agony, going, "OOWW, OOWW!" I tell them to go check him out. Everyone runs over there and leaves me. So now I'm trapped in this wheelchair. I say, "Uh, could *one* of you can come back and help me?"

Later, the stunt double was riding the motorcycle up the ramp, but when he got to the top, he fell off. He was upside down, and the motorcycle fell off with him and landed right on top of him. I was the first one there and, with Eddie the zombie–like strength, I lifted the motorcycle off him. You know how you get this extra strength when you're tested? Later on, I couldn't do it again.

After I moved the motorcycle, everybody ran over there, but the stunt man wasn't moving. Didn't open his eyes. Didn't budge. We were all panicked. We thought he was dead. All of the sudden he opened his eyes, looked around, and he moved his hands, and then he moved his feet. He was all right. They got the motorcycle back on the ramp and he started running around like nothing happened!

Coming attractions

Remember how I wanted to make a music video at Motown? I don't know what they called them then. I don't think they called them anything! Anyway, I get to Epic and start in on them. Before the record comes out you should do this, uh, promo I guess we called it.

I got in touch with Lou Adler and asked him if we did these promo things would he agree to run 'em as trailers in front of the *Rocky Horror Picture Show*. Then I went back to Epic and convinced them to shoot four songs from *Bat Out of Hell*, "Bat," "Paradise," "You Took the Words Right Out of My Mouth" and "Two Out of Three Ain't Bad"—all four of 'em in one afternoon! "Paradise" became a trailer to *Rocky Horror* for a year.

Rocky Horror came out in '75 and bombed, but over the next two years, it started its midnight run in New York, and then it had a midnight run in St. Louis, and people started going. In two years it went from a complete bomb to cult phenomenon.

Wrong fork

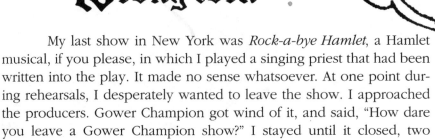

My last show in New York was *Rock-a-bye Hamlet*, a Hamlet musical, if you please, in which I played a singing priest that had been written into the play. It made no sense whatsoever. At one point during rehearsals, I desperately wanted to leave the show. I approached the producers. Gower Champion got wind of it, and said, "How dare you leave a Gower Champion show?" I stayed until it closed, two weeks later.

Around this time I got invited to a fancy lunch party at Kevin McCarthy's house and was sharply reminded of my humble origins. I ventured out of my little one-bedroom apartment on Seventy-fourth Street and headed over to Park Avenue. There was a handful of famous actors and writers drinking cocktails—E. G. Marshall and Kurt Vonnegut, among others. David Rabe was there, also an avant-garde painter, a writer whose novels I'd heard of, a celebrated ballerina, the conductor of the New York Philharmonic—and me.

Dinner is being served, but I'm not sure I can eat.

'Cause I'm from Texas, ya know? I'm a Wolf-brand-chili and barbecue-in-a-can and gravy-and-toast man, and these are major hitters. I'm the singing priest in an all-singing-all-dancing *Hamlet*. I'm going, "Whoa!" The food is being served and they have all these forks and spoons and knives of all shapes and sizes laid out in some mystical order. The whole shooting match.

Leslie, my long-suffering wife, has taught me the proper ettiquette. Like which is the soup spoon. Don't slurp. How to get your napkin right. Leslie has got that all down. Since I don't know what I'm doing, I figure don't do *anything*. I just keep passing on all the food. Better safe than sorry.

That was the first time I ever saw anybody serve sorbet in the middle of the meal. I thought the meal was over. I ate it thinking it was dessert. All of a sudden, they throw down some chicken or something. I'm looking around thinking, "Oh man! *Now* what do I do?"

Later that day, someone asked me, "Where were you?" and I told him about all the people who were there. A whole bunch of stars and me. What the hell was I doing there? I still feel that way most of the time.

PLAYBILL

MINSKOFF THEATRE

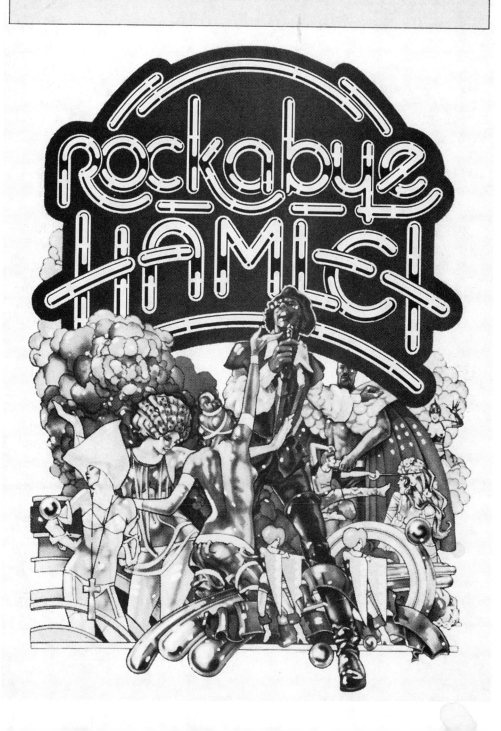

PART

PART 3

bat out of hell

Steinman's brain

When I first met Jim Steinman, he was sharing an apartment somewhere around 102nd Street with I don't know how many people. There were magazines and newspapers piled on every surface, junk stuffed in every nook and cranny. Jim's bed was in the kitchen. He had a rollaway cot; its headboard was the refrigerator. I said, "Jim, what if anybody wants anything in the refrigerator?"

"Believe me, no one wants anything in the refrigerator."

My curiosity finally got the better of me, so when he went into the other room for a moment, I scooted the bed back and opened the refrigerator. It looked like a psychedelic jungle. There were all these colored strands—green and yellow and blue—running all the way

from the top to the bottom, like extraterrestrial vines. Through the nest of frozen vines you could just see a milk bottle. I went, "Whoa!" and slammed the door, hoping no one would ever open it again.

I've often wondered if all that alien life inside the refrigerator didn't have some effect on Steinman's brain. He slept next to it, he dreamed next to it. Perhaps that refrigerator was the source of Jim's later eccentricities. Nah, he was always nuts.

Eventually Steinman moved to this apartment on Eighty-sixth Street. He packed all his stuff in boxes, and I helped him move. I put all those boxes on the floor of the new apartment, and there they stayed—unopened—for eight years. Not only weren't they unpacked, they hadn't been moved from where I left them. Steinman hasn't changed. Even as a multimillionaire he still has boxes, *those same boxes*. In 1983 he moved into a house in Putnam Valley, New York, and those very boxes were sitting in the living room. Still packed the way I had packed them thirteen years before! He had never opened them.

Anyway, one day we were sitting on those boxes in front of his science-project refrigerator when I had an inspiration.

"You know what we need, Jim? A duet. I wanna do a duet. With a girl. Maybe a guy and a girl in a car making out and the girl is telling him to stop." Then I told him the story about me and Rene Allen out at the lake and how I never managed to score. Jim loved the image of the guy and the girl in this car at night by a lake. He burrowed off into his cave to write "Paradise by the Dashboard Light."

Í was john belushi's double

Bat Out of Hell was germinating a long time. Jim and I had been working together since '72, and by the end of '74 we started to get serious. In 1975, Jim sat down and wrote "You Took the Words Right Out of My Mouth," and then he wrote "Bat." At that point, I decided I wasn't going to do any more theater! I was just going to work with Jim, and we were going to pursue our music. Of course, as soon as I decided I wasn't going to do theater anymore, I ended up in another show.

The *National Lampoon Show* was opening on Broadway, and they needed an understudy for John Belushi. When John was asked, "Who can understudy you?" he said, "Meat Loaf."

I'd met Chevy Chase and John Belushi back in 1972 when they were doing *Lemmings* down at the Village Gate. Belushi and I had since become friends. He was a wonderful maniac.

I was at a movie one night and John saw me sitting several rows in front of him. He could easily have gotten up and walked down the aisle to say hello. But, nooooooo! He *crawled*. The movie theater was full, but he crawled on his stomach down the aisle and grabbed a hold of the bottom of my leg. Scared me half to death.

They offered me five hundred dollars a week to understudy Belushi. I said, "Okay, if I don't have to come down to the theater."

"You don't have to," they said, "because John'll never miss a show" and he didn't.

Eventually, they asked me to take the show out on the road. I said the only way I'd do it was if they'd take Jim Steinman as the piano player. They agreed. Jim and I were busy working on the album, and we really needed the money. Because of the musicians' union, he ended up making more money than I did.

Ellen Foley was singing in the *Lampoon* show, so that's how we met her. "Let's do that duet in 'Paradise' with Ellen," I said. It was when we were out on the road doing the *Lampoon* show that things really started moving ahead. In the afternoons, Jimmy and I and sometimes Ellen Foley would work on the songs. We would play the piano and sing songs. And gradually out of the songs came the fantastic characters of *Bat Out of Hell*.

urgatory

When the *Lampoon* tour ended, Jim and I concentrated on getting a record deal. We were rejected by every record company in the world. Four times, at least.

We didn't make demos. We went into recording company offices and *sang*. Live. You can't demo these songs; you either have to record them or do them live.

Jim would play piano and I'd sing. Sometimes Ellen Foley and Rory Dodd would sing backup, but sometimes it was just me and Jim. These meetings were pretty much in and out of there in twenty minutes. Without fail, they'd turn us down. It was fun, though, especially the reactions. We'd be singing along and these record company guys would be sitting there openmouthed. Aghast.

The best would be when Ellen would go with us, and we'd do "Paradise," and Ellen and I would start making out in the office with Steinman doing the play-by-play. "There it is. A line shot up the middle. Look at him go." Not exactly that, because he wrote that especially for Phil Rizzuto. But something similar and we'd just start making out like crazy—she was my girlfriend at the time. It made people uneasy. We were freaks to them.

Making the rounds was like some form of purgatory. Day after day in these grim, fluorescently lit offices with these time-serving dodos.

As we'd walk down Sixth Avenue after these meetings I'd rage on to Jim, "These fucking record company guys are so set in their ways, I can't even imagine how many people they've turned down. Their strategy—always—is to create a formula, make a mold, and then stamp out replica bands. They're really in the packaging business, they just don't know it." Jim would just laugh.

Thinking back on it, one of the reasons we got rejected so frequently was our attitude. These people were used to seeing musicians crawl into their offices, all humble and obsequious. They liked to see you vulnerable and at their mercy. They wanted to be the ones in charge. We didn't come in going "Oh golly. Oh gee whiz. Please sir, what do you think?" I didn't ever play the quiet musician type. That would be playacting!

After a while, we decided we were gonna find a producer and cut some tracks and then take it as a package into these meetings. Producers would shake their heads at us and say, "What do I *do* with this?" It was beyond them.

Everybody was telling me I should be in a rock band and trying to get me into one. Mick Jones was forming Foreigner at the time and he said, "Forget this show tune stuff; try singing with us for a bit."

Couldn't do it. Jim was my man.

Around that time, someone from Epic called me up on the phone and said, "Look Meat, Ted Nugent's having a feud with his lead singer, Derek St. Holmes. Would you come down and finish Ted's album?" This was *Free For All.* I'd known Ted at that point for eleven years, from the days back in Michigan, so I said sure.

They sent me over the tracks and the lyrics. Just lyrics and track, no reference vocal. What the hell was going on? I had to figure out where to sing, where the chorus came in, and all that. Problem was, I'm not really good at that. Anyway, in the end I sang eight songs in forty-eight hours straight. At one point I sat in the studio and sang for seventeen hours. I could sing forever then, never lose my voice. Just sing, sing, sing.

Ted was so pleased he said, "Why don't you come out and do the tour with me?' I went out to see his show and when I saw that on stage Ted was a larger-than-life character himself, I said, "I don't think there's room enough on that stage for both of us."

"You know what?" he said. "You're probably right." I stuck with Jim.

When we went to record companies, people would invariably ask me why I was hanging around with that weird guy.

"And what are these *songs?*" they'd say. "These are not rock songs. Nobody wants a ten-minute song." Well, everything we *did* was ten minutes long.

"These songs are too long, you need to cut them down to three minutes, blah blah blah." I remember people telling me I should be singing R&B, not this Broadway-musical stuff.

But Jim, bless his twisted little heart, kept saying, "The *last* thing you should be doing is R&B. All they're telling you is the obvious. We *know* you can do R&B." His attitude was always, "Let's go against the obvious. If you go against the obvious, it's going to be much stronger."

The reason I believed him was the reaction we got from that song "More Than You Deserve" every time we'd go out live. I'd worked in live bands and nobody ever reacted like that.

reno sweeney

Steinman and I decided we'd go out and perform the songs live. So we put together a band and got a gig at Reno Sweeney opening for Genya Ravan.

We were some sight. I wore a tuxedo, Jim was in his leathers—black leather jacket with studs, black leather gloves with fringes. He used to come out and start playing the piano in gloves. He would smash the piano as hard as he could; it would make his hands bleed sometimes he hit it so hard. He would just start hitting it with these gloves till he put it out of tune. He'd smash the hell out of it. It was very startling and great fun to watch. It made me laugh like crazy to see this guy go at it like he *hated* that piano. Sometimes he would walk out dead center stage and just stare at the audience in his mirrored shades. Then, slowly, he'd take his gloves off one finger at a time. He'd wind up with one glove hanging out of his mouth, then he would go over and smash the piano barehanded.

First time up I began to sweat like crazy. It was streaming into my eyes, I was dripping. My friend Armand Coullet came to see the show and saw what was happening. "You know what?" he said. "You should take a scarf with you and keep it on stage." He gave me a red bandanna, and I still use a red scarf to this day.

When we performed at Reno Sweeney's, we did "Bat Out of Hell," "You Took the Words Right Out of My Mouth," "For Crying Out Loud," and "Heaven Can Wait"—maybe thirty-five minutes—as an opener for Genya Ravan. People went crazy. After the second night, Genya says, "I can't go on right after you guys. You've got them all in a big tizzy." She started waiting half an hour before going on, to let people have a few more drinks and calm down.

Even way back then I knew from the reaction that people would love *Bat Out of Hell*—if it ever got released—would be huge. The following week we were headlining and Reno's was mobbed. They took the tables out, people were standing up, people were crammed into the bar—almost two hundred people. Legally, it held

about a hundred. It got so crowded that several nights they had to pull the gate front halfway down to tell people there was no way to get anybody else in the place.

I wanted the record company guys to come down. I said, "Let them see what's happening here. It'll blow their minds!" Well, they came. And they *hated* it. They'd see the huge reaction from the audience and they'd say, "Oh, you've got all your friends here. That's the only way you could get reaction like this."

"What are you talking about?" we said. "We don't know these people from Adam. We don't *have* any friends." But they were convinced—because the audience was small—that we'd packed the house. We went on to play Carnegie Hall, and just on the basis of word of mouth from Reno Sweeney and a little thing on WNEW, we completely sold it out. It was insane. We had every top executive in the world eventually come down—and everybody to a man turned us down.

Earl

One good thing did happen during that time. We got a publishing deal for the songs, which was a huge help during our years in the wilderness. This came about through Earl Shuman. Earl and Peggy Shuman are sort of my adopted mother and father. They have been friends with Leslie, me, and the kids for twenty-some years.

One morning in 1974, I answered the phone. "Hello?" the voice said. "Meatball?"

"This is Meat *Loaf*," I said.

"Oh God," said the caller, "Of course. I'm sorry."

"That's okay." I told him, "I knew who you meant."

It was Earl. He came into my life through my friend Rhonda Coullet. Earl was a songwriter. He wrote "Hey There Lonely Girl" and "Cathy's Clown." He wrote "Left Right Out of My Heart" for Patti Page. He'd written songs for Sinatra and Dean Martin and Brooke Benton. He had a lot of hits. Rhonda had been making demos for Earl and, when she got stuck, she recommended me.

I went to see him. He'd written this song for Sinatra called "The Bridge." The arranger, Pete Diangeles, had made a beautiful track for it with French horns and strings and I sang it. Apparently, when Sinatra heard it he said, "I can't do this song. The guy who's on the demo owns this song." After that I said to Earl, "I guess I won't be doing any more demos for you."

"I don't think so, Meat," he said.

I brought Jim over to meet him, and when Earl heard the songs, he got us a great publishing deal. We got quite a bit of money for it— forty thousand dollars. Jimmy and I split it between us. It was a huge payday, twenty thousand dollars apiece. That was an amazing day!

Meeting the arch fiend

Jim and I finally got an appointment with Clive Davis, who was the head of Arista Records at the time. At about nine-thirty, nine forty-five in the morning the phone rings.

"Hello, Meat Loaf?" the voice said. "This is Clive," he says. "Listen, soooo sorry, but I've been called out of town, I know we had a meeting this afternoon, but I'm going to have to cancel our appointment today."

I was shaking. All I could say was, "Ye-e-ss sir, okay sir."

I called our manager, David Sonenberg. He says to me, "What do you mean he canceled? I just spoke to him two minutes ago. You guys are on for four o'clock. Be there!" I was confused. Did Clive Davis have amnesia? Had I imagined the whole thing?

What we usually did if we had a meeting was meet an hour earlier at a rehearsal room and warm up. I'd sing and Jim would play for about half an hour and then we would go to the meeting.

Clive Davis's people first put us in a freezing air-conditioned room. I'm going, "My throat. My throat. It's too cold in here." Then the son of a bitch made us wait an hour and a half. I kept saying to Jim, "Let's go. Let's just get outta here."

And Jim goes, "No. No. It's okay. It's okay."

Finally, we head for Clive's inner office. We sing maybe two songs; that's as far as we get and he's already shaking his head. "What are you two *doing*?" He turns to me and he says, "You're an actor. Actors don't make records. You're like Ethel Merman. You're like Robert Goulet. Ethel Merman and Robert Goulet don't make rock records. You belong on a Broadway stage." Now, I'm really pissed. But here comes the kicker.

He turns to Steinman and says, "Do you know how to write a song? Do you know *anything* about writing? If you're going to write for records, it goes like this: A, B, C, B, C, C. I don't know what you're doing. You're doing A, D, F, G, B, D, C. You don't know *how* to write a song."

And then he starts really laying into Jim, "Have you ever listened to pop music? Have you ever heard any rock-and-roll music?"

And Jim, at that time, knew every record ever made. Jimmy is a walking rock encyclopedia. He knew everything, even obscure stuff, like the B side of "Surfin' Bird." And Clive Davis had the nerve to sit there and tell him, "You don't know anything about rock. You should go downstairs when you leave here, go to Colony Records, and buy some rock-and-roll records." Jimmy just kind of laughed it off—that's his nature. He finds insults funny. I don't.

We get down to the street. We're on Broadway around Fifty-seventh Street, and I'm so caught up in my rage I don't know that anyone else exists. I was so angry at this man that in the six o'clock rush in New York, I'm screaming towards the top of his building, "FUCK YOU CLIVE!!!!! FUCK YOU!!!!"

That rejection was the one that sent me over the edge. I was no longer stoking the fire with coal. I was stoking the fire with Kryptonite. I became bound and determined to prove all these idiots wrong.

Later on, I run into Belushi down at the Blues Bar. I'm in the middle of venting about Clive Davis when he stops me. "That's funny," he says, "I thought I'd canceled that appointment."

Getting bat out of hell

We spent most of 1975 auditioning the record. In fact, we basically spent two and a half years going around playing songs for these people and being rejected.

People at record companies hated it. They didn't just dislike it, they were *incensed* by it. I didn't fit their rock-star mold and Jim didn't fit the standard pop-writer role. It was as if we were aliens—starring in *It Came from the Theater.*

And then along came Todd Rundgren. When Todd heard the songs, he rolled on the floor laughing. "I've *got* to do this album," he said. "It's just so *out there!*"

Nobody else could figure out how to record these songs. People kept saying, "Well, how can you make a record out of *that?*" Todd didn't even seem fazed by it.

"No problem," he said. "You just need a deal."

For a while there, we'd tried to get the guy who produced Kiss. He'd done some Alice Cooper stuff, and Jim thought he could do it. I wasn't so sure. But Rundgren, I thought, could. Rundgren had produced Grand Funk Railroad and he had given them their first hit— and I really liked what he'd done with it.

We told Rundgren, "We are all set. We are signed to RCA." We went up to Bearsville near Woodstock to start recording. We were there for a whole month in 1976 cutting tracks. We rehearsed. We got Roy Bittan and Max Weinberg, the piano player and drummer from the E Street Band. Todd brought in Kasim Sultan, Roger Powell, and Willie Wilcox, who were all members of Todd's group Utopia. Todd played guitar. It was all Utopia and two E Street Band guys. Edgar Winter came and played the saxophone on "All Revved Up."

Todd knew exactly what to do. He turned everything around. He didn't have any problems with the record whatsoever. Todd just went, "Okay. There it is. Okay, we are going to move this here, move that there." Like on "Bat," we slow down, we speed up. "Crying Out Loud," "Paradise" do the same thing. Nothing ever stayed to tempo. It makes it more interesting. People who are into dance music obviously don't like it—you can't really dance to it.

After a while Todd wanted to know when the money was coming from RCA. We said, "Oh, it will come. It will come."

And then Rundgren went on tour to Japan and when he got back he said, "Well, we can't go back into the studio until you sort this out." But by then, we had put down two or three tracks. Luckily, David Sonenberg found this guy who owned a bunch of truck stops in New Jersey to put up $150,000 to buy out our contract with RCA and we were rolling again.

Steinman loved Phil Spector (so did Rundgren). That whole wall of sound thing. I originally hated the way it was used on "You Took the Words." Now I love it. What I objected to was the simulated sound. With Spector, the backgrounds are way back inside the wall. The lead vocal is up front, and everything else was behind it. Whereas in "You Took the Words," the backgrounds were not buried back in the wall, they were also right up front. They also had me triple-track the vocal. Boy, I hated it. I thought that was for singers who couldn't sing.

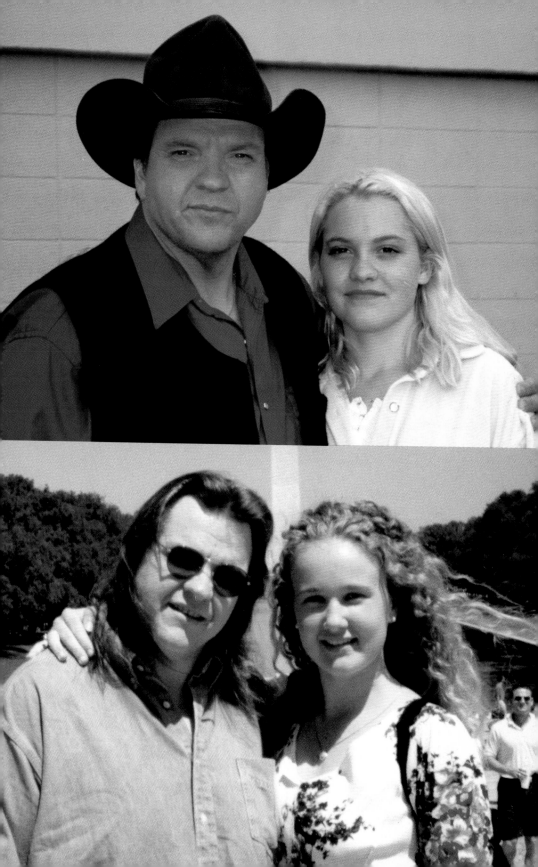

MEATLOAF

♰hantom blonde

Roger Powell had the first synthesizer I had ever seen. It looked like an old switchboard operator's board. Whatever sound you wanted you had to patch in. One day at the house we had rented I asked him if I could play it. He said okay. I was sitting up on the balcony playing the synthesizer when all of sudden, I look up and see a teenage girl run across the whole length of the balcony—past a whole row of windows. I don't think anything about it. I keep playing the synthesizer.

The rest of the band are all downstairs playing pool. When I go down I say, "Did you guys see that blonde!"

"Where?"

"She was running across the balcony," I said.

"How did she get up *there*?"

"Well how did you get the equipment up there? Isn't there another set of stairs?"

"No. We brought it up through the house."

"Just go up there. There is a teenage girl hiding up there." We all went up. No one there.

Later that night I was in my bedroom on the second floor—with the big bed. Jim had the room next door. He wanted a little bed, because that is just how he is. I'm lying in bed watching television with the door partly closed. All of a sudden, I hear the door opening. It makes that creaky sound, because it is an old house. I go, "Jimmy?" No answer. It's winter and absolutely freezing and I'm under a blanket, a quilt, a big bedspread, and a sheet. Suddenly my covers fly off like someone is standing at the end of the end of the bed and ripping them off me. At first, I couldn't speak. I am lying in this bed, trying to scream. Finally, I get it out. "Jimmy! Jimmy! Jimmy!"

He comes in. "What happened?"

"The covers just flew off my bed by themselves."

"Cut it out," he says.

"Jim, I swear!"

I'm scared to death so I get Jim to sit in a rocking chair next to the bed—he doesn't sleep anyway. I was so scared I actually considered asking him to get into the bed with me. I finally fall sleep and he stays up watching TV. I wake up at nine in the morning. He is still asleep in that chair.

Finally, they tell me that the Bearsville accounting office is haunted by ghosts from three different eras: an old man, a young boy; about nine or ten years old, and a blonde teenage girl. So I did see a ghost, but it didn't look like a ghost the way you usually see them depicted. It wasn't transparent. It looked like a regular person running across the balcony. I believe people see ghosts all the time, but they don't know they're ghosts, because they look just like real people. I was able to stay in that room for the rest of the time we were recording, because Jimmy told me that he was taking the ghost into his room and I would be okay now. Jim had a child's toy that mooed when you turned it over. He told the ghost to get into it and then ran to his room. Every few minutes, I could hear this toy mooing from his room, It was Jim's way of telling me he had the ghost under control.

Okay, you want a motorcycle

Rundgren was the one who put all the arrangements together. He took the feeling and made it into a record. We knew how we wanted it to sound; Jim could even hear all the instruments. But Jim doesn't orchestrate, he hums.

One of the most mind-blowing moments in my musical history was watching Todd Rundgren play the solo in "Bat Out of Hell." I don't think I have ever been so amazed at *anything*. He said, "Do you want a solo on this?" Picked up the guitar and did it in one take and one take only. Jim said he wanted a motorcycle sound effect on the track. Todd goes, "Okay, you want a motorcycle, here's a motorcycle."

He plays through the first half of this song, and he gets to the motorcycle part he goes over to this guitar rack with all the bells and whistles—the first one I'd ever seen—and he twists and bends these knobs.

"Motorcycle it is!" he says. And using a whammy bar, without missing a beat, he goes *rrrrrrrraaaaaaaaahhhhhhhrrrrr (first gear) rrrrrrrraaaaaaaaahhhhhhhrrrrr (second gear)* and opens that motorcycle sound straight into the solo and plays it out. He played it all the way to the ending and then went back and said, "Well, that's that."

Straight out of his head. No rehearsal, no practice runs, nothing. I have seen guitar players toil over these things days, hours, a week! Splicing things together. In fifteen minutes he played the lead solo and then played the harmony guitars at the beginning. I guarantee the whole thing didn't take him more than forty-five minutes, and the song itself is ten minutes long. The most astounding thing I have ever seen in my life.

all mixed up

Eventually Todd found out we were not on RCA. We weren't on *anything*. He said, "Okay, listen. I'll take this record now. We got this far and I am going to start a label—so it will be on my label, Etheric." Well, that label never got started. Then Albert Grossman, who had been Bob Dylan's manager, came along, "Okay, well, I'll take this record and put it on my Bearsville label," he said. But when Albert saw that it was going to cost more money than he wanted to spend, he went to Mo Ostin at Warner Bros.

Rundgren said, "Why don't you and Jim do your songs for Mo Ostin." Mo Ostin was impressed. "This is great. I've got to get some people down here to see this." No problem!

Then Todd mixed the whole record in one night. He started at six o'clock and finished at about four o'clock in the morning. In ten hours. But that is not the record you hear. Todd didn't have a twenty-four track in his house, he had a sixteen track. So he ended up mixing eight tracks of drums down to two, which is something you don't do. You don't pre-mix your drums, because then you don't have any leverage to turn up the snare drum or move anything.

About seven o'clock in the morning, Todd says, "Okay, let's go to Sterling Sound. We are going to master." Jim and I were totally dazed, standing there holding this record. We are going, "Wait—these mixes aren't right!"

The next morning we drove to Sterling Sound and mastered

it. And it was horrible. It was awful. "Paradise" was dreadful. I didn't want it on the record, it sounded so horrible.

We next got a hold of Jimmy Iovine—he'd mixed "Born to Run"—and we all went out to the House of Music in Orange, New Jersey, to start re-mixing it there. Jimmy Iovine mixed "Two Out of Three Ain't Bad" and "All Revved Up with No Place to Go," and tried to mix "Paradise," but it was still terrible. His mix of "Bat" was very weird. It sounded like a power trio. It was missing a lot of the elements that Steinman originally had in the song.

Through Iovine we found John Jansen, and it was he who eventually wound up mixing "Paradise," and it is his mix of it that's on the album. Jansen, Jim Steinman, and I mixed "Bat Out of Hell." Jimmy still didn't like it, because it was missing a guitar part—one little tiny guitar part didn't get loud enough. Everybody got a shot with the engineer in the room by himself. The final mixes were all four of us sitting in a room with the engineer, and everybody had different faders. Iovine had drum and tambourine and bass, Steinman had the vocals, and I did the guitars—I wanted the guitars up.

"Paradise" almost didn't make the record. I wanted to throw it off, because nobody could mix it properly. Nobody! Finally, Jansen went in all by himself and came out with it, and I said, "You know, that is great."

Um, jim, what do you think we should call this album?

Jim and I were coming back from Bearsville to New York one evening when the subject of the album title came up. Earl Shuman was driving and trying to stay well out of the debate. We drove into Manhattan, down from 181st Street to the George Washington Bridge to Ninety-sixth Street, where we were going to drop Jim off, and the whole city was dark. It was the blackout of the summer of 1977. Jim wanted it to be called *Jim Steinman Presents...* or something like that. I mean, Jim was not that short on ego exactly, and fancied himself as the mad creator of this whole project—Dr. Frankenstein. Earl, as the voice of sweet reasonableness, was telling Jim that the record company didn't want to confuse the situation, "They know Meat's the performer. They know that he's the, ya know, the voice. And so that's what they want it to be. They wanted it to be *Meat Loaf, Bat Out of Hell*. It's simply a marketing thing, Jimmy."

Naturally this did not sit well with Jim. Jim wanted it to be *Jim and Meat*, like a buddy show—Sam and Dave, Flatts and Scruggs, the Righteous Brothers. Or even *Meat and Jim*, I think he would have accepted. He wanted his name up there; he wanted to be as much of a focal point as I was, and I understood that. We had done it together. But the realities of the music business went against it, and ultimately it was decided to be *Meat Loaf, Bat Out of Hell. Songs by Jim Steinman*. None of this was my doing—or my wish. But it drove a little bit of a wedge between us, and that was probably the beginning of our ambivalent relationship. Our tour manager, Sam Ellis, used to call it "a love-hate relationship that you gotta love."

ı́s there anyone left who can fuck?

Mo Ostin at Warner Bros. told us that his people wanted us to come out to LA. Mo got all the honchos at Warner Bros. together in one room so Jim and I could do the piano vocal thing that we do. I said, "Oh God! I have done this for so long, how can I do this again? But, if it means that much, okay."

Ellen Foley, Rory Dodd, Jim, and I went over to Warner Bros. We were going to do the whole album—piano and voice with some background vocals. The room was full of people—thirty or forty people.

We do "More Than You Deserve," "Paradise," and a few other songs for them. The performance is going well, everybody seems to like the songs and it looks like we're a shoo-in. We're going to get the deal! Jim and Meat on Warner Brothers! Jimmy has a strangely maniacal look on his face, but with Jimmy that could be anything.

I don't know what's going on and I don't find out till the next day. An irate Lenny Waronker tells Sonenberg the deal is off, Sonenberg tries to get us another shot but Waronker is furious, "I'll tell you one thing for sure," he says. "This record is not coming out on Warner Brothers. I will not have that maniac on my label." And that was that.

I'm walking down Sunset Boulevard with Jim, and I tell him that Warner's has turned us down with a vengeance. They practically want to run us out of town they're so mad.

"We've had some pretty extreme reactions, but this definitely takes the cake," I say.

Jim thinks this is funny. He thinks anything said to him that is in the least bit negative is funny. It seems to just roll off him.

I'm going, "What got them so upset? You don't think it had anything to do with me and Ellen Foley making out during "Paradise' do you? I mean you'd have to lead a pretty sheltered life to be outraged by that."

"Oh, don't take it personally."

"How can I *not* take it personally? From what Sonenberg reported to me, it sounded like hanging would be too good a fate for us."

"Yeah, they did the same thing to me when I auditioned *Dream Engine* for them."

"You *know* these people?"

"Yeah, I know Lenny Waronker. I went to him and Jack Nietzche four years ago to get backing. Jennifer Warren was there, too. Before I'd even gotten through the last verse, Jennifer Warren leaped up in a fury and said to me, 'How can you write such filth? That was the most disgusting, vile music I have ever heard in my entire life. How can you call yourself a human being?' Then Lenny Waronker got up on his hind legs and started shouting, 'I want you to leave my office. *Now!* I don't ever want to see you again!'"

"Uh oh, what was the song?"

"'Who Needs the Young.'"

"You *didn't?*"

Jimmy has an instinct for getting to people. If you're trying to get backing for your musical and the backers are easily-offended, middle-class people, "Who Needs the Young" is not the song that's going to win them over. I love it. I wanted to put it on *Bat*, and one day it will get on an album, but it's a seriously abrasive, ghoulish song—in the tradition of Bertolt Brecht and Kurt Weil. A black comedy German cabaret song. It goes something like, "Is there anyone left who can kiss? Spit on 'em. My sex just isn't what it was. Is there anyone left who can fuck? Screw em!" I think it is the most hysterical song ever, but apparently Jennifer Warren and Lenny Waronker didn't share our sense of humor.

We'd been unceremoniously been given the bum's rush by Warner Brothers. What were we going to do now? We'd finished the record. The contracts were all done. The lawyers were unscrewing their Mont Blanc pens. We were supposed to sign the next morning and have our pictures taken for *Billboard*. The whole thing blew up in our faces, all because of one itty bitty obnoxious little song!

Now, David Sonenberg who was our manager at the time was scrambling. He'd represented the E Street Band on a couple of contract negotiations, so he called up Little Steven—whom I know and most people know from the E Street Band as Steve Van Zandt or Miami Steve—and he gets Steve to call Steve Popovitch at Cleveland

International Records. He'd heard *Bat Out of Hell* and liked it, but was undecided.

Popovitch was a promotion guy who could get stuff on the radio. He walked around with a boom box everywhere he went, playing stuff. He didn't give you a tape to take home and listen to. He played it for you on the spot. Steve Popovitch thought Miami Steve was the genius in the E Street Band. I probably wouldn't argue with him on that. Little Steven told Popovitch that that little fifteen-second interval at the beginning of "You Took the Words Right Out of My Mouth" was the best intro in the history of pop music. Little Steven convinced him that *Bat Out of Hell* was going to be a hit.

A couple of days later he called Popovitch again and said, "Hey, you got one last chance!" Cleveland International had been the other company we were courting. It was a new company—the only act they had on the label so far was Ronnie Spector! We played this game that we were getting ready to sign with Warner Bros., but we would really, really like to be with Cleveland International because we said we thought Warner Bros. was too *big*.

Sonenberg got Popovitch coming back around thinking that we were going to sign with Warner Bros. "Look," says Popovitch, "This has got to go to Cleveland International. You'll have the same deal, only you'll have us *working* for you."

Eventually we said, "All right, all right. We will go with you guys instead of Warner Bros." We didn't, of course, have a hope in hell at Warner Bros.

Bat Out of Hell came out October 21, 1977, on the Cleveland International label, which at that time was affiliated with Epic and CBS. And pretty much everybody at Epic Records hated the record. I mean, really hated it. The head of marketing threw up his hands. "I just don't get it!" he said, and tossed it into the ocean off Cape Cod.

meat loaf TO HELL AND BACK

the meat loft

As we started thinking about a tour, people were asking me what we were going to do for a road manager. I said, I know a guy, he's in the theater. He's a theater stage manager, but he's the guy. I know he can do it. That was Sam Ellis, who I knew from *Rainbow*, and he turned out to be an incredible road manager.

It was the summer of '77. We began to get ready for the tour. The preparations all took place at the Meat Loft. It was an eighth floor space on Eighth Avenue and Thirty-fifth Street, which is right in the middle of the Garment District in Manhattan. This is where we rehearsed and had our offices. We started holding auditions, looking for people to be in the band.

At the same time, we were still going out to the House of Music in New Jersey to re-mix the record. We held auditions in the afternoon, then out to the studio till four in the morning. Then back in town, auditioning more musicians. You know, just putting the whole thing together.

Ellen Foley had sung on the album and the record company wanted Ellen to do the tour, but it just didn't work out. Ellen had a great voice, but it was critical if *Bat Out of Hell* was to work on stage that the girl who played opposite me be a great actress. When I saw Karla Devito, I knew that this was the girl.

We kept late hours because of Jim's habits. His mattress was in the closet, because he slept all day long. He never got up before four o'clock in the afternoon, unless something really really really important was happening, which was almost never, according to him. He slept in a closet because that was the darkest, quietest place to sleep during the day. Six, seven in the morning—that's when he goes to sleep, just like a vampire. Gets up at four or five when the sun starts going down and gets back to work. Recently, he told *Entertainment Weekly* that he's sleeping upside down in a tree in preparation for writing the Batman musical—and you can almost believe it.

Susan Blonde was the press person at Epic. I remember having lunch with her at the American Steak House and saying, "I am not doing anything without Jim Steinman. I will not do any interviews for this record without Jim Steinman being there. I won't take any pictures without him, I will not go to any radio stations without him. It's a project. It's me and Jimmy." At first we did everything together, if we went to WMMR in Philly, we went together. WBCN in Boston, WNEW in New York, WMMS in Cleveland.

Eventually, I had to do it on my own, simply because Jim couldn't keep up the pace. At some point, he started to bail out of things, saying, "I am too tired, I can't do it." For him to travel anywhere, to get on a plane and go to California or go to England, was a major production. He physically couldn't do it. Turns out I shouldn't have kept up that pace, either. But more on that later.

those kids are here to see you

As *Bat Out of Hell* was being released, the record company asked me who I wanted to open for. "I'm not an opening act," I told them. It wasn't arrogance, it was self-preservation. 'Cause I'd already been in a band that opened for Rare Earth, and my shenanigans eventually got me thrown off that tour. It didn't work with Genya Ravan, either.

"You got to open for somebody," they insisted. "We'll book you into Chicago—we're going to have you open for Cheap Trick." Okay fine, whatever you say.

We went into Cheap Trick's stomping ground, their home turf. *Bat Out of Hell* had just been released. Nobody knew what the hell we were doing. Jim Steinman had had these costumes made that were the most bizarre things in the world. What Karla was wearing was so extreme I've just blocked it out of my brain completely. Jim got us all in these funny getups and everything, floppy hats that hang off to the side, and he's going, "It's great, it's *so* great." I wasn't so convinced.

"Jim, what *is* this? This is not going to work." Jim, however, is thrilled. To him it's full-blown *theater*. He's incredulous that I should even question what he's doing.

"What are you talking about?' he says. "This is going to blow them away." If they don't blow *us* away first, I think.

Jim looked at *Bat* as theater, and to a certain degree I did, too. Rock with theatrical *elements*, sure. But it's got to be a *rock 'n' roll* show first and foremost. If we go out there trying to be some off-Broadway theater of the absurd, we're going to fall flat on our faces. But I let him do what he wanted. What did I know?

So we walked onstage to this Cheap Trick crowd—nothing but Cheap Trick fans as far as the eye can see. And nobody applauded. Not one clap. Nothing. I walked out and got in front of the mike, and right then a guy in the front row stood up and said, "Fuck you, you fat son of a bitch, get off the fucking stage!"

And I looked at him, I pointed at him the way I do, gave him the Meat Loaf face, and I said, "Okay, you asked for it!" We started to play, and by the time we'd finished the first song—we opened with "Bat"—they were still booing and hollering and giving us the finger.

And the guitar player passes by me, I've got my back turned, and he says, "Meat, this is bad, man, we should just get off the stage while we still can."

I looked at him and said, "Shut up. We agreed to play for forty-five minutes and you better just start fucking playing." That's my basic instinct.

By the third song they're still freaking out, standing up and jeering. Yelling "Fuck you," "Boo," "You jerks!" About thirty minutes into it, things are cooling out. They didn't exactly like it, but by the end of the show nobody was calling me a fat fuck, either. I considered that a victory.

Times had changed, and this was typical of the seventies. In the sixties, nobody booed anybody. You might not get such big applause, but you had acts of very different stripes all playing together. Richie Havens playing with the Who, you had Ravi Shankar sitting there playing the sitar with Blue Cheer! People didn't even boo *Yoko*. In the sixties, you just didn't go there. It didn't make any difference what the band was playing, people would just sit and enjoy the music. Nobody said, "Fuck you, I'm gonna *kill* you!" It took me years to get over that show.

A couple of days later, we pulled up for sound check at a club in New Jersey and saw all these people standing around, just hanging out. I was wondering who they'd come to see. I go inside and everybody is staring at me.

"What do you have going on this afternoon?" I ask.

"Hell man," they say, "those kids are here to see you."

"What?" They were lined up *in the afternoon.*

Bat Out of Hell had been released two days before the Cheap Trick concert. By the time we got to New Jersey, just two days after that disastrous concert, everything had changed for us.

The place was mobbed. The feeling was overwhelming, of being at the edge of some huge wave about to break.

There's a photograph of me on the back of *Dead Ringer*—my hair all down and me all sweaty—which was taken at the second show of that Jersey gig. That picture, to me, is a picture of the night we made it. A moment of pure, unadulterated amazement and joy. At a little club in Jersey.

 he moment

Soon we were a success. In New York—and Cleveland. We had Scott Muni in New York on our side, and of course Cleveland International had Cleveland sewed up—Kid Leo at WMMS. But nothing much was happening anywhere else.

"You Took the Words Right Out of My Mouth" was the first single off the album, and it wasn't doing what everyone thought it would. There was some resistance at the record company, of course, because it was too theatrical. They didn't know what to do with it. But we were out there doing live shows and everyone was loving it. And we were selling records wherever we performed. Slowly it started getting more and more air play on the FM stations, but the moment when it crystallized for the record company was in New Orleans where CBS had its convention in January 1978. Walter Yetnikoff was there, all of CBS, and Epic. Plus Billy Joel, Elvis Costello, Cheap Trick, Mother's Finest, Ted Nugent.

We were the last act to go on. I was so into "Crying Out Loud," that when I finished, I had my eyes closed. Now normally when you finish a song, the audience will start applauding. But the room was silent. It felt like an eternity. I'm standing there with my eyes closed expecting applause but hearing absolutely nothing. Two or three seconds after the song is over, there's still nothing. I had enough time to think this one thought: "They've all left." That's how long it was. On stage, a moment is an eternity.

I'm sure my face showed real fear during those few seconds of "Oh my God, they simply *left.*" Because that song is a nine-minute song. We start with piano and voice, and then the band comes in, and it ends with piano and voice. The ending itself is a good two minutes of piano and voice. At the end, I take the mike away and it's just my voice cutting through the theater.

And then, as I started to open my eyes to see the awful truth, the room exploded. They stood up and started to scream.

They were yelling and whistling and climbing on chairs. There were people standing in the middle of the big round dinner tables. All for a damn *ballad*. That night, and singing the National Anthem at the 1994 All-Star Game, are the best moments of singing I've ever had in my life.

Of course, when you've got them to that point, you don't let 'em go. You don't stop and *talk* to them; you punch them in the head. I turned around and I looked at the band. "Johnny B. Goode"! was all I said. The lyrics fitted the situation perfectly: "Deep down in Louisiana, close to New Orleans. . ."

As soon as we began playing "Johnny B. Goode," people started running up onto the stage. There must have been two hundred people on the stage while the band was still playing. There are pictures of the audience at this moment taken from the stage looking out, and you can see the whole place standing on the tables and all these people on the stage and the band all looking like deer caught in the headlights. We were that stunned. People were jumping and dancing and carrying on. They went crazy, completely berserk. Billy Joel was standing on a table. They were throwing chairs. They did something like forty thousand dollars' damage to the room.

They told me that the only other person who ever made such a splash at a CBS convention was Janis Joplin. Which is the best compliment I've ever had in my life. And that night set the wheels in motion. Whether they hated *Bat Out of Hell* with a passion or not, they finally got behind it.

{they don't make hotel walls the way they used to

The night after the CBS convention, we were meant to play this little club in New Orleans. During the day, we went there for a sound check—the bar was open and the owner was there. The stage wasn't big enough to get us all on. So the crew had built this little extension. They'd gotten the wood and constructed a new stage.

A drunken redneck at the bar comes up and glares at me.

"You got any niggers in your band?"

"Excuse me?"

"You heard me, boy."

"What?"

"You playin' with me, boy?"

"And if I am?"

"Ya know what?" he says. "If you come back tonight, I'm gonna shoot you. And that little dark-haired beauty over there as well." He was pointing to Karla Devito.

He said he was going to blow us away, and I believed him. I did not doubt him for a second. So it got to be around eight-thirty, time for the gig, and I wouldn't budge. I'm telling Sam Ellis and everybody, "I'm not going back there. I'm not doin' this show. This guy said he's gonna shoot us, and I think he just might. He's that ornery."

They go, "Aw, c'mon, Meat, he's bluffin' ya."

I told them, "You guys weren't raised in the South. None of you. You weren't raised down here. I was. And this is New Orleans. New Orleans is the crookedest town in the whole world. It doesn't get any worse than this."

"Well, whatever," they were saying, "you should still play the gig."

"No way am I going back to that club."

"You've got to play this gig," Sam is saying. "We *contracted* to play these gigs."

"I don't care if you made a contract with Don Corleone," I say, "I'm not going!"

"No, no, no. You gotta go. You gotta go."

All these people were in this room telling me I gotta go. I realized I had to make my point a little more forcefully. I walked into the bathroom. I was really angry, and I rammed my head against the bathroom wall a couple of times, and the second time I did it, my head went right through the wall. It was the cheapest plasterboard you could get. I'm lucky to have missed the stud. But my head sailed right through the wall out into the bedroom where everybody was sitting. Concussion number seventeen.

Sam just looked at my head covered in plasterboard poking through the wall and said, "Yep, okay. We're not playin'."

But that wasn't the end of it. They put out a warrant for us. Said we stole their mike stands and their microphones. That's how crazy and crooked New Orleans is. The guy who owned the bar? His brother was the *sheriff*. On top of all this Mardi Gras was starting. Everyone's even crazier than usual. Three o'clock in the morning we were trying to cross the street, get through the paraders and the Mardi Gras floats to get a hold of Sam to warn the band that the police were after everybody. They went to all our hotel rooms and went through our luggage. We were damn lucky they didn't find anything in our suitcases.

By six-thirty in the morning, we were at the airport. Time to get out of Dodge.

{they're playing
our song

The two things that really helped us get rolling were *Saturday Night Live* and the radio stations.

I was good friends with John Belushi and Gilda Radner, and due to their pushing us and John's loud mouth, they finally got us on *Saturday Night Live* in '78. The show was critical for us because if you went on *Saturday Night Live*, the next week your record could sell anywhere from fifty thousand to one hundred thousand copies—bam!

But when the time came I was absolutely petrified. I thought I was going to pass out. John and Gilda had to do everything in their power to calm me down.

We did "All Revved Up," and at the end of the song I ran at the camera and made this Meat Loaf face like, *"You come on!"* John loved it, he thought it was "sooooo great!"

By then radio had kicked in. Bob Putnam at WNBC played it and the Night Bird, Allison Steele, was playing it, too. The first time I ever heard it on the radio was at midnight and on her show. I called everyone up, "Hey, I just heard 'Bat Out of Hell' on Allison Steele!"

I was so happy when Top 40 radio in New York played " Two Out of Three Ain't Bad. That was the first song they played. Then they discovered "Paradise." Soon, the rest of the country followed suit. I was ecstatic.

Even the magazines that didn't like the record liked our stage show. Jimmy was in that first *People* magazine article—Jim and I talking about how we created this record together. Somehow that comaraderie would get lost along the way.

$tolen words

We went up to Toronto to do a show. We were big in Canada. More people in Canada owned *Bat Out of Hell* than owned snowshoes. I got Jimmy to come up for that show. While we were on stage, somebody broke into our dressing room. They stole all kinds of money and our guitars. But these were replaceable. What was really disastrous was that Jimmy had brought his lyric book with him—with all the new lyrics for the next album. They stole that, too. This was the album that was going to be called *Bad for Good*. That very night, we were going to sit down and start going through these new lyrics. The book never surfaced. That was a huge, huge setback. I think that really was a terrible reversal for him. He had written all these songs and worked really hard, and when he lost that book I don't think he ever completely got it back. That's where the second album disappeared. I think some of the songs he got back. "Left in the Dark," "Renegade Angel," and "Surf's Up" are a few of them, but he could never, ever get them all back in his head. After that, he sank down in the deep end. The blow was devastating for him and somehow that second album got lost there.

Steinman toured with us until June, then he went home to write lyrics. But it was while on the tour that something happened that was to affect him for the years to come.

"Jimmy, what's the matter?" I asked.

"Nothing, nothing."

But I can tell right off if anything's wrong with anybody. If they say "Nothing," I push it out of them. You can ask my wife—Leslie hates me when I do that. She says I'm the one who insisted on getting it out in the open. Finally he turned and said to me, "I hate you." Woo!

"I'll tell you why. Because when you walk down the street everybody knows who you are. When I walk down the street, nobody knows who I am and we started this together."

"I agree with you," I said. But I didn't know what to do about it.

While the rest of us kept on touring, the record company came to me and said, "We want to put 'Paradise' out, but we're getting resistance from the radio stations because it's so risqué. We need you to go out and promote it."

I learned more about the music business in the month of September 1978 than I ever wanted to know. I saw with my own eyes what the promotion guys went through. The radio station guys say, "Yeah, we should be playing your record. We're not, though."

"Why not?"

"Well, because we want something from you."

"What do you want?"

"You want us to play your record? Then you play our concert. You play our December radio jamboree, we'll play your record, *capisce?*"

Now I'd go, "Sure, let's do it." But back then I thought it was absolute blackmail. I thought they were putting a gun to my head and I'd go, "Well, *fuck* you! You should be playing my record just because it's good, not because I'm doing you a favor." I mean, to me this was no different than payola. Which we were *already* paying. I was asked to sign a check for one thousand dollars, to some interior designer in New Orleans!

The Dr Pepper Festival in August 1978 was wild. The crowd went crazy. They climbed on the limos—it was like Beatlemania. One fan got so excited, she went right through the roof of a limo. *Melody Maker* called us "the worst band in the history of rock 'n' roll." Pretty impressive, eh? What that did for *Bat Out of Hell* was extraordinary. It caused the album to increase in sales by leaps and bounds. All the press came out just to see the worst band ever, and ended up spreading the word. All the way down to South America, the Middle East, Israel, and Greece.

Bat Out of Hell began to sell, but it took forever. We didn't have any money from October through July and we were out on the road the whole time. I find it hard to believe at this point that we were advanced over two million dollars in road expenses by the record company—but that's what I recall being told. My lifestyle was very minimal. I had a couple of pairs of jeans, this funky leather jacket that I'd had since Detroit, and my apartment, the rent for which was around $285 a month. I wasn't exactly having suits custom-made or buying Tony Lama cowboy boots.

It wouldn't be that hard to spend two million dollars on the road by today's standards, going on an arena tour with lights, equipment, crew, and so on. But this was twenty years ago and we weren't doing anything like that. We were playing clubs and theaters. Our set was minimal. We weren't even carrying our own lights. I didn't buy a lot of stuff for myself, but I did spend a bit of money on my friends and relations. I loved my Aunt Mary, and I bought her a car. I lent people money. I bought people cars. Kind of like Elvis, but not Cadillacs. More like Fords.

]jow i got in the baseball hall of fame (sort of)

Jimmy had always said, "You know what we need in 'Paradise by the Dashboard Light?' We need to get a play-by-play thing in the middle there, like the old thing we used to do in school: getting to first base with a girl, second base, a home run. That type of thing." He wanted it to be a real baseball commentary, with a twist—a double play of sex and baseball.

First, we thought of Mel Allen and then we went, "no, no, it's gotta be Phil Rizzuto!" Because back then he was really on top of his announcing game. He really had it together. "Holy cow, I think he's gonna make it!"

We called up his agent, who turned out to be Art Shampski who'd been right fielder for the Miracle Mets of '69. The big line to come from the Art Shampski meeting was this, "So, listen, Phil is thinking about doin' this thing, but he's got one question. He wants to know one thing. Do people have to get stoned to listen to this record?" Jim looked at Art Shampski and smiled and said, "Ya know what? I think that with this record, it's probably it's better if people don't."

So now we make a deal with Rizzuto to do it. It's one of the great moments of *Bat*. But getting there . . . man! As soon as Phil enters the studio, our problems begin. We're wild tracking it, which means there's no track. We just have him record it and we'll fit it in. It was summer, so we listened to Rizzuto call all these baseball games, got all his dialogue together—the kinds of things he would say. He really wrote it. We just kinda edited it and put it together for him.

He got in the studio and he couldn't do it. It's not that easy to play yourself. He'd go, real monotone, "There-it-is, a-line-shot-up-the-middle. Look-at-him-go. This-boy-can-really—"

"No no, Phil," we're saying. "Like you do it during a game!"

"That's what I'm doing."

Next take he was a little bit better, but it was still pretty deadly. I'm thinking, maybe he needs to see the game, maybe that's why he can't do it. So I went out into the studio and ran the bases to fit with what he was announcing. Around the music stand, over to the piano, around the drum kit. Pantomimed him hitting the ball and running to first, rounding first and I slid in the studio floor, I slid into second base, acting it out for him. And he got it. And once he got that, we played it back and he said, "Oh! I see!!" He did it a few more times and then they edited it together.

But ever since then, Phil has been saying how much trouble he got into with his priest down the street. And Catholics "all over the world." Meanwhile his kids who were in college up in Boston at the time, loved it. They were such heroes at school, cause their dad was on the "Paradise by the Dashboard Light" record.

Wherever I went after that, I'd tell anybody who would listen that Phil Rizzuto should be in a Hall of Fame. I don't think we hurt him, because sixteen years later he was inducted in the Hall of Fame. And, here's the great thing. Behind Rizzuto's plaque at the Baseball Hall of Fame in Cooperstown is a CD of *Bat Out of Hell*, a baseball hat that says MEAT LOAF on it, and a guitar pick. The guys who were putting the hole in the wall for the plaque put it back there.

They asked me when Phil was going to be inducted, is it okay if we use "Paradise by the Dashboard Light" at the ceremony? Are you kidding?

But whenever Phil gets on the radio he says, "That huckleberry Meat Loaf got me in more trouble with that song." Four or five times in a season he'll say it. "That darn huckleberry got me in more trouble with my priest and all the people on my block and all the Catholics around." Whenever he sees me he says, "Meat, you're some huckleberry for getting me to do that."

I say, "Phil? You love it, you know you do." I mean, if he didn't love it, he wouldn't keep telling the story, right?

(how i got to be larger than life

I'm asthmatic. I was a lot bigger back then, and I still get winded on stage today. I've learned how to pace it now, I have musical breaks in there. But in the early days, I'd keep going right straight through—like the record, plus all my ad libs and improvs. As well as our own songs, we did really demanding stuff like "River Deep, Mountain High." We played mostly in small smoky clubs. Being asthmatic, I'm really allergic to cigarette smoke and I was completely winded every show. We needed to have an oxygen tank by the side of the stage. I was sixty pounds heavier than I am today. I would just collapse at the end of the show and they'd have the oxygen there for me to breathe.

It became a traveling road show. And all my shenanigans and my passing out became something people had to see. Sam Ellis would administer the oxygen and immediately I'd pop right up. It turned into a riff, like James Brown with his cape.

"Live at the Bottom Line" was broadcast over WNEW and it sounded like a prize fight. They broadcast both shows—back-to-back double shows at the Bottom Line. At the end of the first show, the deejay goes, "He's down! He's down!! Oh my God, they are giving him oxygen. Wait, wait, the rest of the band is stepping over him like nothing is wrong." There were pictures in *People* magazine showing me passed out on the floor and John Rosbrooks, the assistant tour manager giving me oxygen. Real James Brown show biz stuff! The new guys in the band were always panicked when they saw it. The other guys in the band would just walk over me as they came off-stage.

One time it happened in Atlanta at the Capri Theater. I was so out of breath I was passing out. It was early in the show. I was pretty sick at the time, and during "You Took the Words Right Out of My

Mouth" I went down. They had to get paramedics in there to revive me. I was totally out of it. And when I came to—there was a woman paramedic giving me oxygen—I thought she was an angel. I really thought I had bought the farm that time. There were several other times when I fell off the stage, but that one was the worst. That one I went completely out—I was sure I'd died.

During one of the shows in Australia—Adelaide—they took a picture of me lying down, passed out on stage with the headline: MEAT LOAF DEAD. I get a call the next morning from the States, waking me up. It's Earl Shuman.

"Are you dead?"

"I don't think so," I said. "Call me back at noon and I'll let you know."

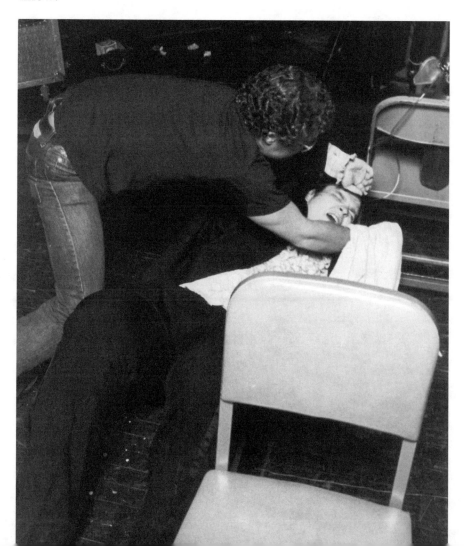

Now i know why sinatra slugged that guy

I think things between Steinman and me really took a twist when we went to Australia in June 1978. The record was so big down there. "You Took The Words" was number one, the album was number one. When we landed it was like the Beatles. You know those pictures of them at an airport and all those people up against the fences? That's how it was when we arrived. It looked like ten thousand people out there pressing against the fence. I remember looking out the window and thinking, "What's going on?"

We went immediately into a press conference. They started asking Karla questions. They were asking me questions. They weren't asking Jim that many questions. They said, "Let's have a photo." I'm saying, "Okay, Jimmy and I will pose for this photo." They were going, "No, no, we want Karla in it as well. Karla, get in the picture." This was just too much for Jimmy. He got really upset when that happened. He didn't come down to the next press conference.

I remember having this picture taken with me sitting on the motorcycle with Jimmy right behind me, and Karla is way in the back. He hated that picture. He understood me getting the attention, because I was the front guy, but when Karla started getting as much attention as he did, Jim didn't like it one bit.

Years before that, Frank Sinatra had gone down to Australia and punched an Australian reporter. I remember thinking, "I can't understand how a guy like Frank Sinatra, a professional who has been doing this so long, would not be able to control himself over some stupid reporter's remark. Well, I soon understood it all too well. We were at a press conference in Australia, everybody was very gracious, we were making jokes and laughing. All of a sudden, this TV reporter pops up. He says, "Hey, Meat Loaf"—thick Australian accent—"when are you going to lose some weight and give us a real show, mate?" When that son of a bitch said this to me, I didn't answer him, I lunged at the press table. I went after him.

Geez! When are you going to lose some weight and give us a real show? Sam Ellis grabbed me and held me back. After that I understood why Frank Sinatra had punched an Australian reporter in the face! Because if they hadn't grabbed me, I would have done the same damn thing.

And then the trouble started

Bat Out of Hell was selling, selling, selling. Everywhere in the world it was showing up number one here, number one there. Every song was a top-ten single in England. It all happened so fast. In August 1978, they were going to present me with a platinum album in Cleveland. By the time they had the platinum album pressed and ready to give to me, it had already gone double platinum—in a week. In August and September, *Bat Out of Hell* was selling over half a million copies a week worldwide. This went on for twelve weeks.

When *Bat* became a success, a lot of people started to feel resentful. In the beginning nobody was upset because *Bat Out of Hell* wasn't doing anything, and then all of a sudden it hit. When people who'd worked on the album saw that, they all wanted something. Jim, by this point, was getting money from the publishing, but I got hardly anything, because, according to the record company, we were in the hole to them for three or four million dollars. How was that possible? The record wasn't that expensive to record. If I'm not mistaken, *Bat Out of Hell* cost around $235,000 to make.

Anyway, all these people were angry. I'd probably been horrible to them, too. I was out of control. I would have tantrums—nightly! I would rage in my cage before going on. I would throw chairs, demolish dressing rooms. I threw microphone stands at the band. I was throwing microphone stands at the *audience*. I was a perfect monster. The band would give me a wide berth as if I were some beast in captivity about to be exhibited to the public.

i am god! you are fools!

As *Bat* got bigger, I got crazier. It was like some terrible curse where everything I'd ever wished for turned into a nightmare, and it was rapidly turning me into a maniac. If I'd had my way, the hallways of record companies would run with the blood of incompetent executives, promoters would be hanged from lamp posts, and the band would suffer the torments of hell. I AM GOD! YOU ARE FOOLS!

And then it came to a terrible head in Arlington, Virginia, when the tape of "Bat" began to slow down on the *Midnight Special* and I ended up in a strange hotel by a lake in Canada. The band caught up with me in Toronto. I'd gotten there three days early and a few brain cells short. Then it was on to Ottawa! I shuddered to think what might happen next.

Well, in Ottawa I fell off the stage and injured my leg. I think it was my way of taking myself out of the situation. The road, the drugs, the drinking, the exhaustion had become intolerable and I had become a monster.

It had been just completely insane from the Cheap Trick gig in October '77 right through to the *Midnight Special* in May of '78. That was the only time that drugs ever came into play. It was coke. I was so worn out and so tired and it gave me that artificial energy I needed. It certainly did not help me, because it led to the nervous breakdown. It got so bad.

I think it had to do with the fact that I was completely out of my mind. I was so driven to prove all of these people *wrong*. Because I was bound and determined that I was right and they were fools. Part of the problem may be that I was so arrogant—but without, of course, trying to be arrogant. Probably it was that drive, that thing that wants to say, "I TOLD YOU SO!" Plus I had a terrible temper.

I drank a whole fifth of something before I went on stage in Philadelphia for a live radio concert for WMMR at the Tower Theater. This is how crazy it got. To get *Bat* played on the radio, I was doing stuff that I would never do now. I would go on morning radio shows, go on afternoon radio shows, do the show. After the show, I'd go do late-night radio. I was working all the time. You get that with the kind of energy I put into my shows. You start going crazy. I was going to make this album happen, whatever it took.

Cocaine has this weird way of making you feel like you are in TOTAL CONTROL OF EVERYTHING. All life and its meaning is crystal-clear in your brain. You have this very sharp perspective on certain things for a brief moment. But it goes away fast, real fast, to where it gets delusional.

I'm told, and I'm sure it's true, that during my nervous breakdown I was out on the ledge of a building in New York. It was like THE END. I was going to jump off. They had police and fire department and everybody there. Sam Ellis talked me down. I don't even remember being on the ledge.

Eventually, I was forced to stop touring. People turned their backs on me because they thought I would never recover—very few people come back from a drug psychosis. But even *without* cocaine, I was crazy. With it, I was even nuttier. That's the way coke works, folks.

This went on for a year. But it was when they took me off the road, that things got really bad.

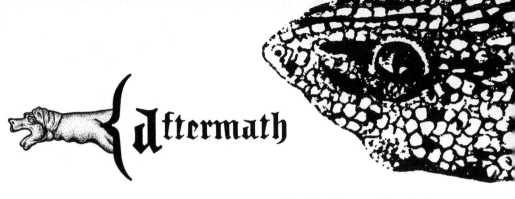

{aftermath

All my life, after a show, I've tried to back way off. I don't want to do anything else. I don't want to go out. I don't want to go downstairs to the lobby. I want to go back to my room and I want to sit there and shed all those characters, let them evaporate back into thin air. I don't want to go out and have somebody talk to me about the show, because that means I'm staying in the space that I want to get out of.

I think the constant pressure in '78 was what really got to me. Because *Bat* was so big and I'd worked so hard to get it there. It was all happening at once after five years of struggle. Cocaine was a way of escaping, or so I thought.

People were constantly coming to me, trying to get me to do things. "You have got to go to this club, Meat, you have got to go here, you've got to do that." And I did.

My obsession with maintaining the tension in the shows was also taking its toll. I was going slowly crazy and I was doing it alone. I wanted to drive Cadillacs into swimming pools, I had orgies with bevies of groupies, I caused scenes in restaurants. I was so crazy that I wouldn't go back to my room.

The pressure was building. I get very intense-looking in photographs and in certain songs, too. Most of those pictures of me looking like a rampaging Ramada-Inn-demolishing maniac come from "Bat," because that's what we used to open with. "Bat" was a very intense song. Or "Paradise," where you see me making the Meat Loaf face with the big pop eyes—being scared of the girl. So the general image of me was this wild man who had to be put back in his cage.

People got this idea that I was a beer-guzzling, biker maniac, and that's who they wanted to see. I got that a lot when I would do interviews. I'd have to slip back into the Meat Loaf character. Now, when I do interviews I take a step back and go, "Wait a second." But back then, everybody had this picture of me screaming like Godzilla—that was my image. Meat Loaf Godzilla. Well, he *is* my favorite character. The old Toho Studios Godzilla is a perfect rock-and-roll character. He's completely goofy. He destroys Tokyo, but he's always falling over.

Sally Field says that "acting is like cutting yourself with razor blades." And that's just what I was doing to myself back in August 1978; I had cut myself to death with razor blades. There was never a moment when we weren't promoting. I was always on. Plus I'm living *Bat Out of Hell* morning noon and night. All those characters constantly swirling around my brain. It was like having multiple personalities.

Remember that *Twilight Zone* episode with Jack Klugman, in which they land on Mars and see a space ship that looks exactly like their ship? They are all dead—they are ghosts but refuse to believe it. They just keep crashing over and over again. "Bat Out of Hell" is like that, a continual loop, a Rod Serling nightmare. The "Bat Out of Hell" character has a face, too. He is a cross between Elvis, James Dean, and Clint Eastwood. Sort of tall, dark hair. Like Elvis and Clint Eastwood put together. The girl is a redhead and the town is somewhere in the Southwest. It is very dusty, a gritty kind of feeling.

"Paradise" is definitely New York. *The Honeymooners.* A cross between Jackie Gleason and Orson Welles. "Paradise" is another vicious circle. These guys live there and they *stay* there. They don't go anywhere else. "Left in the Dark" is actually a woman. "Heaven Can Wait" is a very old man. The room he's in is always white. I am not sure if he is in a hospital, or where he is. He may be dead already, for all I know. Those were the characters I had become.

In October I hung around in New York. The record was so big that I couldn't go anywhere. I went back to my apartment on the first floor. The window was just high enough to see into and there was a high school across the street. People would be outside the door all the time. I was always good with the fans and interacted with them. I've always been really easy to approach. People would start talking to me as if I knew them, as if I'm their next-door neighbor or their brother. But I couldn't stay there anymore. There were twenty people constantly sitting out there. So I went to the Mayflower and I didn't leave. I sat there, pretty much through October, I believe. Eventually they had to break the door down.

Dr. frankenstein's revenge

Jim and I finally saw each other in November. We had a little office down at Thirty-eighth Street and Eighth Avenue. We had a piano down there and we were working together and everything was fine. All of a sudden, after Thanksgiving everything changed. We were supposed to get back together but I lost track of him in December. Dave Sonenberg had signed him to a management deal by this time and nobody was telling me where he was. Eventually, I found him. He was up at Roy Bittan's house in Woodstock.

Deep in my heart, I started to believe that Jim wanted everybody to believe that he was Dr. Frankenstein and I was the monster. Without him, perhaps I'd fall flat on my face.

Where have you been for the last three hundred years?

In December, still in pretty wobbly shape, I went up to Woodstock to work on *Bad for Good* at the Bearsville studio. Leslie Edmonds was the assistant studio manager there. She was a beautiful flower child with perfect porcelain skin—a bit of a beatnik, someone who'd been around the music scene for years but, like myself, felt disconnected from it.

Part of her job was to find the band members places to stay because we were going to live up there while we were recording. She drove me around to look at the different houses we could choose from. There were apartments over the studio. There was a house at Turtle Creek that had three separate apartments in it. There was another one called the Cummings House. It was around the corner from the Bear Cafe. There were apartments over the accounting office. I picked the Cummings House. Richard Manuel from the Band was living in one side of the house and I got the other side.

While looking at these different houses, we ended up spending a lot of time driving around together, and we fell in love almost immediately. In a matter of days. It was kind of scary and crazy at the same time.

It was like looking in the mirror. I saw my other half, my soul mate. I looked at her and I saw something in her face—it was like, "Where have you been? I have been looking for you for three hundred years." We were both looking for the true loves of our lives; we both wanted a family and children.

But it was also very immediate, and a little frightening. I asked her to marry me about a week after we'd met. I'm sure a lot of her friends were asking her, "You mean that fat sweaty guy on television? Why are you doing this?" I could see she was terrified to marry somebody so soon after having met him. And I was afraid this was the big moment in my life and I somehow knew in a very deep sense that if I didn't ask her to marry me right then I would be sorry for the *rest* of my life. At a certain point I was more afraid *not* to do it than to do it.

We were at the Cummings House. There was a blizzard outside. The wind was howling, snow was blowing against the windows, and like a man possessed I turned to Leslie and said, "If you won't agree to marry me, I'm going to cut my beating heart out with a carving knife and throw it in the snow." This might have sent some women running out of the house. But not Leslie. Whether it was true love or her fear that she might be responsible for a bizarre form of suicide, she agreed to marry me.

At this point she knew almost nothing about me. Now *I* was nervous. She'd never heard any of my records or seen me act. What if she hated my music? Up there in Woodstock she was in a very insular music situation, outside of the artists who recorded at Bearsville. She didn't listen to the radio. She didn't go to concerts. I wanted her to like what I did. I took her to a record store and bought her a copy of *Bat Out of Hell.* We took it back to the house she shared with blues harmonica player Paul Butterfield—they were housemates. She had the downstairs bedroom area and he had the upstairs.

Paul was out; he usually was. He didn't spend a lot of time at home. He hung at the bars a lot and came home and slept it off and got up the next day and went back to the bar. I came over, played *Bat* for her. When the record finished she said, "It's really . . . different. And beautiful." Well, I'd passed the first test. Now I wanted her to see me in the *Rocky Horror Picture Show.* I had a video of it and we went back to the Cummings House where there was a VCR. Jim was sitting in the kitchen when we got there. I was saying to him, "What if she hates it? What if she hates what I do? What if she hates my singing? What if she hates my music, my movie, my acting?"

Jim laughed. He has a ghoulish sense of humor. "Who wouldn't love Eddie the brain-dead zombie?" he said. I needn't have worried. I was her knight in shining armor who was going to take her away. And she certainly was a damsel in distress. Her life in Woodstock had been, up till very recently, that of an indentured servant. She would look after people's houses, drive people around, and cook for them, do their laundry, look after their children, and they'd give her room and board and treat her horribly. All these rich rock stars and their managers. She was working twelve, fourteen hours a day, seven days a week. Finally she got a job as an assistant studio manager at Bearsville making a whopping $120 a week. She had a daughter named Pearl—after Janis—who was almost three, who went to the Montessori school in Woodstock until three o'clock and then she would sit in Leslie's office and she would play with blocks and color for the last three hours until it was quitting time. She was such a good child.

It was a fairy tale in the middle of a nightmare. My life was in turmoil and Leslie's was not much better. I came to town and saw how hard her life was, trying to raise her child and getting caught up in the negative aspects of Woodstock in 1979, a lot of drugs, a lot of drinking, a lot of partying. I got into huge screaming arguments with Paul Butterfield and Albert Grossman about the way they treated her. Meanwhile they were all furious I was going to take their servant away from them. They were giving her all these reasons why she shouldn't marry me. They were trying to talk her out of it. I said, "I'm going to get you out of here. I'm going to scoop you up on my horse and ride you out of town and get you out of this hellhole." And we never looked back.

I wanted to make everything wonderful for Leslie. Shortly after we met, we went down to New York to see a play. After the theater, we were walking down Fifth Avenue and past a shoe store. I could see Leslie's eyes were as big as saucers as she looked at this amazing pair of shoes in the window. She was from Woodstock, she had only two pairs of shoes to her name, and at the moment she was wearing Army boots. But these incredible, shiny, blue metallic, lamé, high-heel, disco shoes were calling to her. She was mesmerized. The next day I had one pair in every color sent to her. Twelve pairs of shoes for Cinderella.

We met around the beginning of February '79 and were married on the twenty-third at Todd Rundgren's house on Mink Hollow Road in Woodstock. We got married twenty-one days after we met. We called everybody we knew on a Wednesday and said, "We are getting married on Saturday. Do you want to come?" They all thought we were nuts. I think something like two hundred people showed up. In a total blizzard. We gave people three days' notice and they came from all over the place. I think people were taking bets as to how long this thing was going to last.

Here we are, twenty years later, and we are still together and each other's best friend. Richard Manuel was there and Eric Andersen, all of my band, and Albert Grossman. Albert was saying to Leslie, "Why are you marrying this guy? He's crazy, you know." Jim Steinman was the best man and Susie Ronson, who was married to Mick Ronson at the time, was one of the bridesmaids. Leslie's parents came and my Aunt Mary, and Earl and Peggy Shuman.

Todd's house was on top of a mountain and it was covered with ice. It was so slippery you couldn't drive to the very top. You had to get out of the car and walk up. Leslie wore a little white shirt-waist silk dress and I wore a brown woolen suit. At the last minute Earl had to rush into town and find some suspenders; my pants were falling down. He managed to find a place that sold them and saved the day.

The minister had to be in his nineties. He was an ancient fellow. I remember Sam Ellis and Don Ketteler having to literally carry this guy up the mountain and then hold him up throughout the whole ceremony. And Todd was taking pictures with his camera, and it turned out he forgot to put any film in it.

There was a large candelabra set up on the piano that cast a beautiful, romantic light across the wintry room. At one point in the ceremony the minister tripped on his long robe, stumbled backward, and the sleeve of his vestment must have caught fire on one of the candles. He was utterly oblivious to what had happened and continued on with the ceremony, declaiming in a quavery voice, "If any here see any impediment to the joining of these two . . ."

No one else in the room noticed at first what was going on because the part of his robe that had caught fire was behind him. But when the frail minister raised his arms in a gesture of benediction the ample sleeves of his robe were sheets of flame. They looked like infernal flaming bat wings. It was such a stunning sight that for a moment nobody moved. There was just this loud gasp of horror. Sam Ellis and I rushed over to him, pulled his robes off, and rolled him on the ground. He was still in a daze when the flames were put out and with great dignity he got up and said, "Shall we proceed?" It was a good omen.

PART 4

PART **4**

paradise lost

 # Play it again, sam

Jim and I had a monster hit album, sold out shows, and aside from the little matter of me having temporarily lost my mind, we were on a roll. Nothing could stop this freight train. All we had to do was make another chart-gobbling album, and follow it up with a sold-out world tour. Right.

Of course, it was just at that moment that everything began to fall apart, as if some fiendish gremlins were jamming the gears:

"You guys think you're just going to repeat your success? Watch this!"

I was mad at Jimmy; Jimmy was mad at me. We fought about everything on the new album. He wanted to use the session musicians who'd played on the first album; I wanted to use our current road band. We fought over songs, we fought over arrangements, we fought over takeout food.

The new album was going to be called *Bad for Good*. When I

got up to the studio in Bearsville I had been upset to find that Jim and Todd had started on the album without me. Apparently, I was no longer to be a part of the creative process. They became very condescending. They handed me the tracks and said, "Go in the booth, sing your part when we tell you to, and go away." Whoa!

One day when we were recording a track with Rundgren, I told him that I didn't like the segue that they were doing. I asked if it could be changed and Todd said, "Like hell!" He then proceeded to say to me, "If you can't speak to me in musical terms, don't speak to me at all. You're just the vocalist, we're not asking for your opinion, so just shut up." I got up and left.

And suddenly, everybody had an opinion of how I should sing. "Why don't you try this, Meat?" "Can you do it softer, Meat?" "Not that soft, Meat."

"It's not *about* singing," I'd tell them. "It's about possession, and it's none of your damn business!" Sometimes I'd throw people out of the studio—bodily.

"I'm a Method singer, guys—can't you understand that? Once I find the characters it'll get easier." They'd look at each other and roll their eyes.

In the meantime, there was unrelenting pressure from the record company. When *Bat Out of Hell* became such a huge success, they started bugging us to come up with another record. And what they wanted—what they *always* want—was the same thing all over again. They're lazy. They don't want to have to deal with anything new; they want you to replicate.

At this point, Jim started creating these *Bat* (and Bruce Springsteen) clones. Songs like "Stark Raving Love" and "Bad for Good." Now the thing that had really nettled us in the reviews of *Bat* were the unfair comparisons to Springsteen. And what does Jimmy do? He writes this song, "Bad for Good," which really did sound just like one of Bruce's songs. I'm going, "Jim, man, what are you doing? All these idiots are saying we sound like Springsteen, and now you're *trying* to sound like him?"

He was trying to copy "Bat Out of Hell," but it wound up sounding like "Born to Run" or "Thunder Road." He tried to answer "Paradise by the Dashboard Light" with a song called, "Dance in My Pants." I don't blame Jim. I blame the record company. The record company was saying to us, "We want to get this album out fast to capitalize on *Bat Out of Hell*." I'm telling Jim, let's not go there. My gut tells me it's too soon. It doesn't work when people turn records around that fast—rarely does it do well. You've got to space it. They played *Bat Out of Hell* so much on the radio that it got burnt. If you have any stick-to-itiveness, you just hold out.

If they would have waited—this was only 1979—Jim and I would have had time to develop a new concept. They would have had another successful album like *Bat Out of Hell*. But all they were interested in was their billing cycle. They wanted the dollars *now*.

I don't know if Jim was naive or simply pressured, but he caved in to their dopey demands. He doesn't anymore. Now he says, "I don't want to do it. It isn't going to get done." When they push those pieces of paper under his nose, his attitude seems to be, "I don't care what piece of paper I have signed. I don't care what kind of contract I've signed. Nobody's ever made me live up to a contract, so why should I live up to one now?"

I was so distressed by what Jim was doing that, on New Year's Day, 1979, I went to see Billy Joel at his house in Manhattan to ask him what I should do. We were watching football and I was talking to him about my concerns—he'd been in the business for a long time. He gave me some advice: "Don't rush it. Don't let the record company rush you into anything. They've got a different agenda than yours."

That conversation made me stronger. I didn't want to see Steinman and me pushed into delivering this next record that quickly and I especially didn't want to make a Xerox copy of *Bat Out of Hell*. Did the Stones try to redo "Honky Tonk Women"?

But these were just theoretical considerations compared to what came next. The unthinkable happened. I lost my voice.

And the lord taketh away

The moment I really flipped (as opposed to just being generally nuts) was when I finally tracked Jim down to Roy Bittan's and found he'd been there for three and a half weeks working on the album without me. By this time I was already pretty far gone—too much touring, too many drugs, not to mention success, exhaustion, et cetera.

Meanwhile, I was losing my voice. Everybody was critiquing my vocals, and now there *weren't* any.

And it wasn't that I wasn't singing as *well* as I'd sung on *Bat Out of Hell.* I couldn't sing, period. When I tried to hit the high notes all that came out were horrible high-pitched noises and squeals.

The doctors all said there was absolutely no reason I shouldn't be able to sing. There was nothing physically wrong with me. I had simply shut down.

At the same time, Jim was off working on the new album with some piano player—before we'd even had a chance to sit down and go through the new material. I was so upset I couldn't even express my disappointment to him.

One night I took a whole bunch of pills, went to Jim, and said, "Jim, I swallowed a bottle of pills." He took me down to the Kingston Hospital near Woodstock and had my stomach pumped. I wasn't really trying to kill myself. I don't think people who are trying to kill themselves show the empty bottle of pills to their best friend right after they take them.

I don't exactly know what I *was* trying to do. Jim and I had been so close for so many years and worked everything out together and all of a sudden I wasn't involved. I'd lost my voice and Jim at the same time, and I was scared.

And now that I could no longer sing, there were quite a few people who had absolutely no use for me. God knows, I'd probably given them a real hard time when I *had* a voice.

"You don't need Meat Loaf," the people at Cleveland International were telling Jim. "You're the *writer*. You can do it all."

These were the spin doctors and movers and shakers who a year ago were handing me a platinum record and telling me I was God almighty. And I believed them!

The entire record business had a straw up its nose, and a mirror on the table with a big pile of cocaine. They were all fucking crazy, and one thing a coke fiend can't do is *wait*. It's the nature of the beast.

Jim came to see me around Christmas of 1979.

"I'm gonna do this record now," he announced. "I'll write you some other stuff, okay?"

"No, Jim, it's *not* okay," I wanted to say. "No one can sing those songs the way I can." Problem was, that I couldn't sing. At all. My voice was simply not working.

life goes on (sort of)

Two weeks after I walked away from *Bad for Good* (or it walked away from me), I got the part of Travis Redfish in *Roadie*, directed by Alan Rudolph. Lots of great people were in it: Debbie Harry, Roy Orbison, and Hank Williams, Jr. Art Carney played my father.

I played a roadie who was really not a roadie; he was just a guy who lived in Texas and was a genius at fixing things. The theme of this movie was everything works if you let it. There are guys I've worked with who always say, "Yep, we can make that work." Nothing is impossible. Then there are other guys who always tell me, "No *way* can we do that."

In the movie, one day Blondie comes down to Texas to do a show, but can't go on because there is no power. So Travis gets his friends to bring in pickup trucks full of cow manure and potatoes and creates a methane generator to make the sound system work. There is rarely a rock-and-roll movie in which everybody isn't a cartoon.

Roadie came out on the same day the *Blues Brothers* movie was released. Let's just say it didn't do too well in comparison.

After *Roadie*, Leslie and I went back to New York. We found ourselves an apartment and tried to figure out what we were going to do next. My singing career was apparently over. You've got to be able to *sing* to be a singer—that's the minimum requirement. Even our good friends weren't too encouraging about my future in rock.

We didn't go out much. Our life became very insular. When we did go out, it was mostly to other couple's houses, like the Belushis, John and Judy. Most of the time, we watched videos. Having Pearl, who was still a small child, you can't stay up all night. I didn't want to anyway. I hated those kinds of nights when we would be coming home in a limousine and dawn was breaking. We had a babysitter and all, but still, when your child is getting ready to have

cornflakes or something and you are just going to bed, it's a bit strange. Embarrassing for a rock singer to admit, I guess.

The only other couple we knew was Billy and Elizabeth Joel. He was another one of those artists like Bobby Darin and Sandra Dee who were very popular but not considered cool. Like me. Elizabeth said, "They talk about us behind our backs, too. They call us Queenie and Dumb Dumb. But what they don't know is, he is Queenie and I am Dumb Dumb."

Pearl loved Billy Joel's songs. She would play them over and over again on her Fisher-Price record player. When he met her at a charity softball game, she was just overwhelmed that he was there. I said, "Come on, Pearl. Let's go and meet Billy. He wants to meet you. Let's go over and say hi."

She said, "No. I want him to come here." She was four years old. Billy came over and knelt down and kissed her hand. He was kind to her, very sweet. Asked her to marry him. He's a very generous spirit.

The early eighties were all disco. We went to publicist Susan Blonde's birthday party at Studio 54 and we couldn't wait to get out of there and never go back. We just weren't into it. We would hang out with the Belushis down at the little blues bar they had on the West Side. It had a great jukebox, with R&B, soul, Motown, and Stax-Volt stuff on it. Everybody who was in town doing *Saturday Night Live* or a show at Madison Square Garden would show up there: Bonnie Bramlett, Levon Helm, the Allman Brothers, the whole Blues Band including Steve Cropper and Duck Dunn from Booker T. and the MGs—they had gotten back together for the *Blues Brothers* movie.

The great thing about the Blues Bar was it was private; it wasn't like going out. Of course, there was a lot of drugs. One night John and I had a competition. We competed about everything. Who'd had more accidents, who was more afraid of needles. This particular debate was about who could do more coke.

Okay, I said, let's test this theory, because you are offending my regional sensibilities. So we laid out one huge line of coke in the shape of Illinois and another in the shape of Texas, and you *know* how much bigger Texas is than Illinois, right? I still won.

You've got to become one with the bat

Leslie and I felt like we'd always been together, but it wasn't so easy for Pearl. It took her a while to adjust. She was almost four, and didn't like me. *At all.*

Our apartment was close to Central Park and I used to take Pearl with me when I went to play softball. I guess I thought it would be a nice outing for her. Hah!

We'd get home and Leslie would say, "How was it, Pearl?"

And Pearl would say, "It was terrible, Mommy. It's just always Meat Loaf, Meat Loaf, Meat Loaf, Meat Loaf, Meat Loaf, Meat Loaf." Out of the mouths of babes.

So Leslie kinda glares at me and asks Pearl what in the world she's talking about.

"Well, everybody keeps coming up," she says. "That's all they want to do. Everybody wants to talk to him."

It was true, that summer there was a bombardment of people coming around. Fans, people I knew from the park. I'd played ball since the summer of '72, and I knew *lots* of people in Central Park. Practically everybody I know, I've met playing softball. The summer of '78 I didn't play that much. This was the summer of '79. *Bat* had been out for a year and everyone wanted to know about it.

My team would play the Actor's Studio in softball. I'd say to them, "I am going to throw the ball to you. Become one with the ball." If they missed it I'd go, "Uh oh! you lose! You didn't stay in the moment!" The Actor's Studio softball team was terrible.

I enjoyed the park, but out in the real world it got to the point that there were so many people coming out of the woodwork, I didn't trust anybody. I developed a phobia about being called a star. I wouldn't allow the publicity people to use the word. They'd want to write, "A brand-new star has catapulted onto the scene." I'd say, "No, no, no! You can't put that in. Say 'an amazing new album' or something. Just don't use *that word*. It makes me crazy." I couldn't handle it.

By the end of the summer, the only time I left my room was to go to Central Park and play softball. The only people I felt comfortable with were the people that I'd known from my acting career and the guys I played ball with—my friends before *Bat Out of Hell.*

And, even there in my sacred space, the baseball diamond, the guys started saying to me, "Meat, you've changed, man, you're not the same guy we used to play ball with."

I'd tell them, "No, don't you say that to me, because I haven't changed one bit. I'm just the same. If anyone has changed, it's you."

"Here," I'd say. "Go bat. I'm pitching, you're the shortstop, you're the center fielder. Let's play ball."

Meat: the dark side

I always had a terrible, awful, horrible temper. Drugs, the road, and a touch of megalomania had only made it worse. I was encouraged to act out. When provoked I could effortlessly call up that Hell's Angel character, and the audience *loved* it. The more mike stands I threw and the more drum kits I kicked over, the louder they yelled. When I pick up a chair I can look seriously menacing. I could be truly terrifying because I was so big and scary and sweaty and long-haired.

But all that had to come to an end once I was married. Domestically, it isn't good—the beer-can-eating, womanizing maniac from hell is not someone you want popping up in your living room in the middle of a domestic dispute. It's like saying, "If I can't have my way I'm going to nuke Lower Manhattan." Leslie couldn't take it. Nobody could.

Leslie understood what I'd been through, because there'd been alcoholism and violence in her family, but for that very reason, she couldn't cope with my outbursts. She would cower in a corner and not speak, which was devastating. The more withdrawn she became, the angrier I'd get. My natural impulse is to bring it all out in the open and scream and yell until we get it solved. Leslie couldn't do that. It didn't take long after we were married for me to learn that I had to put the monster back in his box when I came off stage. Leslie has taught me this new motto: The first one who raises his voice loses the argument. She won many, many arguments that way.

Meanwhile, I was still trying to straighten out the problem with my voice. The doctors all said, "Meat is fine physically. It's all mental." But psychosomatic or not, I still couldn't sing. I even went to a hypnotist but I have no idea what happened there. Maybe he woke me up like they do in the movies, saying, "You will remember nothing." On my way out the door he tried to convince me that everything was okay, but when I got to the studio I was still totally terrified. And with good reason. Nothing worked. We played Ping-Pong instead.

People kept telling me about this magical healer named Warren Berrigian. James Coburn swore by him—had this guy *living* in his front yard, in his movie trailer. Berrigian had also treated Jackson Brown and Cheech Marin. The phenomenal Steve Vai told me, "Yeah, we went to Warren. He's from another planet. He does these weird exercises in which you go into these trances and black out and things from your past start coming out." I was dubious. But desperate.

Warren was like a kindly old mad-scientist grandpa. He had very weird ideas and even stranger ways of treating people. His therapy consisted of having me lie down on the floor and sing notes while he vibrated a Black & Decker hand sander with a sheepskin pad on it against my leg and my knee. His theory was that I had become traumatized when I fell off the stage and broke my leg on tour in '78, and had short-circuited the electrical circuits in my body, and this was the reason I couldn't sing. What he was trying to do was to reconnect the circuits—using power tools!—and it worked.

Time, Leslie, and a better frame of mind also helped bring my voice back. I got off drugs, I played softball. I tried to forget about everything.

total megalomania

Jim was doing *Bad for Good* by himself, but what did I care? I had my voice back. In 1980 I began work on a new album, *Dead Ringer*. Steinman wasn't involved at all, other than writing the songs and handing them to us.

The guitar player on the session was playing the lead solo to "I'm Gonna Love Her for the Both of Us," and right there in mid-riff he ODs—as we're recording! He just keeled over, slumped down, and all of a sudden you heard this *nyeeeebhhh*. Hey, nice sound!

"What's he doing?" We knew about his problem and we'd told the roadie, "Whatever you do, do not give him drugs. Period." Roadie went right out and scored for him. We had to take him to the hospital. Lead guitar players, they're all out there on the Planet Stratocaster, trust me.

We had an arena tour coming up to promote the album. For the *Dead Ringer* tour, we built a huge set with some wild props. We had an amazing illusion for the opening number, "Bat Out of Hell." I went to Rick Baker, who is the number one special effects artist, and had him make a face and body mold of me. I then put them on Freddy Galfus, the assistant tour manager, and had him dressed like me in a tuxedo and red scarf. When "Bat" started, Freddy (who now looked exactly like me) would appear at the top of a riser holding the mike as if he was about to start singing. Suddenly, smoke would go off and he would fall through a trap door onto a stuntman's landing bag. At the moment he landed, the lights would go on again and I would pop up right on the front of the stage and begin singing.

Just as we were ready to hit the road with this extravaganza, it got mysteriously canceled after one show at the Brendan Byrne Arena in New Jersey. My manager, David Sonenberg told me it had been canceled from lack of ticket sales. I called a promoter in Maine and asked him about it. He said, "I didn't pull out of the show at all. I have a nine-thousand seat arena. It's now seven weeks before the date and I've sold seventy-seven hundred seats. I am going to sell out. They told me you canceled the show."

Then I heard a new story: "Oh, the record company only advanced $200,000 and it's all spent." This came as something of a surprise to Walter Yetnikoff, who told me CBS had actually advanced twice that amount.

It was around that time that David Sonenberg had come to me and asked if he might transfer half of my management contract to a gent named Al Dellentash. I gave him my consent. Dellentash leased planes to celebrities. They called him "Helicopter Al."

Sometime back, I had signed a five-year management contract for a significant percent of my income to go to David Sonenberg. He was clearly a very shrewd guy and Jim swore by him.

You could tell that Sonenberg was smart, but once Dellentash came on board strange things started to happen. Certainly they were an odd couple. Sonenberg was this baby-face guy with pretty little features, blond curls, and little round glasses. He wore sloppy linen blazers like the Harvard lawyer that he was. Dellentash favored the slicker, Italian shmooze look. Despite these sartorial differences, there was a shrewd meeting of the minds.

The music biz was apparently just a sideline for Al. He would tell these stories about flying to Libya with a load of automatic weapons. Or landing in a field in Spain with no one around and just emptying the plane—dropping the goods in the middle of a field in some old prop plane and taking off. They were entertaining adventure stories, and I hadn't a clue if they were true, but they sure were enough to make me afraid of him. The moment Dellentash entered the picture, everything seemingly went to hell. And it all happened overnight.

Sonenberg and Dellentash would get as much money in advances from record companies as they could. Money for albums, money for tours, money for movies.

They got advances for a tour that ended after one show. Much of that money apparently disappeared. They got advances for a film, and some of *that* money disappeared. Around the time they also acquired a townhouse on Riverside Drive for use as an office.

They were spreading themselves a bit too thin.

I don't know if it was cocaine or incontinence, but it looked to me like nobody in that entire office could sit at his desk longer than ten minutes without going to the bathroom. Al would get up in the middle of meetings and disappear for days. I could never figure it out.

I came to the conclusion that everybody in this building must be high on *something*. It was total megalomania.

We were recording *Dead Ringer* one day during the New York cocaine blitz of 1981, when Dellentash came into the studio. Everybody was talking at once. He'd brought in a shoe box wrapped in tinfoil and put it on the Ping-Pong table. It looked liked a present on which the wrapping had been ripped open. I opened it expecting to see cookies. When I took the tinfoil off I saw it was full of hundred-dollar bills. Wrapped like in the movies, with the little seal around them. It was in ten-thousand-dollar bundles, and the shoe box was stacked full. I said, "Whoa!" and wrapped it up again. Fast.

Al said he had an offshore company he was using to beat the IRS. They were putting this money in this offshore company and from time to time he would send guys down there with cash. That's why it was wrapped as a present. With all the stories he told, I scarcely knew what to make of this one.

With Dellentash in the picture, everything was done on a grand scale. He and Sonenberg weren't just going to make a record—they would make a movie based on the record (and at the same time spin off a bunch of videos while shooting the movie). Big plans made on glass coffee tables.

Meat loaf to the power two

Dead Ringer was going to be a Meat Loaf movie. They proposed the idea to Sony and got CBS to put up a million and a half to make it. Alan Nichols was going to direct it. They said they were going to open a big production office. Now that they were movie producers, they had to have an office worthy of their new status. They went Hollywood in a big way. For the premiere of Foul Play, Dellentash flew Chevy Chase, Henry Winkler, and me out to LA in the Rolling Stones' jet. The townhouse on Riverside Drive was furnished it in the most lavish style imaginable. Sonenberg and Dellentash were giddy. They were just like high school kids—you have all the answers and whatever you say is funny and everything you do is cool. They were continually thinking up these wild projects. The office was palatial and incredibly furnished—with Louis XIV desks and antique mirrors. A huge gold lobby. Everything paneled. And a pink room: Everything in it was a pale, pale pink, including the grand piano. It was going to be the Party Room. There was going to be the Serene Room. They hired a chef who prepared these elaborate meals. Crazy plans blew through the office like whirling dervishes. Dellentash was building a big fancy house in Jersey somewhere with a soda fountain and a jukebox, like a drugstore from the thirties. The spending escalated daily. It was just pie-in-the-sky craziness all the time, and no real attention to what should be going on.

Every idea they had was "Genius!" Everything was the next huge big deal. The movie itself was part and parcel of the ongoing megalomania. In the *Dead Ringer* movie I played myself—twice! Meat Loaf and Meat Loaf's biggest fan. Josh Mostel played the biggest fan's brother.

The plot involves a contest to see Meat Loaf. And as his biggest fan, I'm following Meat Loaf around. The biggest fan in the world is really shy. He doesn't speak and he walks funny, but when Meat Loaf gets sick he comes out of his shell and replaces Meat Loaf in his own show. While we were shooting the movie, we did a whole lot of videos; it was ahead of its time.

I did a duet with Cher in the movie (and on the album). It was shot in a bar with all the softball team guys standing around drinking. There were scenes around swimming pools with nude girls. It was an ongoing party, and while I was shooting the movie, they wouldn't tell Leslie where I was. Although Leslie is gorgeous, they wouldn't allow her or Pearl to play themselves. They wanted actors to play them instead. It wasn't that Leslie couldn't have done it, it was because they were fostering the separation. Al Dellentash and David Sonenberg were seriously trying to split us up. They gave my ex-girlfriend Candy Darling—a real girl, not the Warhol superstar!—my phone number, just to make Leslie crazy. They were doing everything they could to split us up.

Leslie was convinced the reason was that with her in the picture, they couldn't control me. Leslie is smart and she could sit back and see what was going on. When I'm working, I put on blinders. To keep me away from Leslie they kept me busy doing this and doing that so that I would never stop to see what the hell was happening.

When Leslie and I were married, David Sonenberg had taken Leslie aside at some point at the wedding and said, "Meat Loaf's appeal is that he has nothing. That he is very basic and he doesn't spend money, that he's not acquisitive and lives a simple life. As his manager, I would really resent it if he were to change his image or his life in that way." It was such a creepy thing to say.

Alan Nichols's version of the movie was shown at the Toronto Film Festival and actually got some good reviews. But that was the only place it ever showed. His version was pretty good, but then Dellentash and Sonenberg took over and started editing it themselves. It turned into a wildly disjointed and jumpy movie—a victim of major self-indulgence. It featured weird scenes with Dellentash and Sonenberg that made no sense. I remember sitting with Leslie in a screening room watching it with all these CBS executives. About thirty-five minutes into it, I just got up and left. I didn't want to be in that room when the lights went on.

* * *

It took Jim forever to finish *Bad for Good*. He was almost a good year in front of us when he started but in the end both my record and his got finished around the same time. When *Bad for Good* was finally ready to be released the people over at Epic found out how genuinely wacky Jim Steinman was. As part of the album's promotion he demanded that Epic buy two thousand stereo systems identical to the one he used—with the exact same speakers and the same amp—and send them out with the CD for reviewers to listen to. He insisted that was the only way they can really hear it. It would have cost an absolute fortune.

Then Epic did the weirdest thing. Not only did they release *Bad for Good* at the same time as *Dead Ringer*, they also put a sticker on *Bad for Good* that said, "The Creator of Meat Loaf."

Steinman was no longer just "The Creator of *Bat Out of Hell*," he was "The Creator of Meat Loaf!" I couldn't believe my eyes.

Our first day in hell

1981 was not a good year for us, but one great thing did happen right at the beginning of the year—Amanda Aday was born on January 21.

It was great when Leslie was pregnant, because I got to use all the fat jokes that had been used on me over the years. *Poor Leslie can't wear Levi's.* I finally had a comrade. When Amanda was born, poor Pearl had chicken pox and gave it to Leslie in the form of shingles. So she had to be quarantined for the first week Amanda was home.

We had the trip to the hospital carefully planned. Leslie's suitcase was packed and left by the door. We're in bed watching the Knicks-Celtics game on TV. Pearl was playing with Colorforms on the floor. It was also the night of the pre-inaugural party for Ronald Reagan and the day before the release of the Iranian hostages, and I hear Leslie saying "Meat, my water broke. I'm going to need new underwear." I start panicking— and not thinking. I rush into the bedroom, reach into my chest of drawers and pull out a pair of huge, white jockey shorts. Pearl is sitting on the bed and says, "Daddy, you silly, that's *your* underwear."

We finally get a cab. There's a blizzard outside. It's midnight by the time we get to the hospital. We'd been to Lamaze classes for the previous weeks and I'm trying to give Leslie moral support by breathing along with her. I'm going, "Breathe! Breathe! Breathe!"

Leslie looks up at me and says, "Fuck you! *You fucking breathe.*"

I'm not a good candidate for witnessing childbirth. If I even *see* a needle in a movie or on *ER* I have to look away. So I sort of watched and I sort of didn't. When Amanda was born she was bright red, like a little fire baby, apparently from all the vitamins Leslie had taken during pregnancy.

When we finally got her home and Pearl was allowed to see her, she sniffed Amanda from head to toe, like a little animal.

Leslie goes, "What are you doing, Pearl?"

"I'm trying to figure out what she smells like."

"And what's your verdict?"

"She smells like MFP Fluoride."

Around Thanksgiving weekend of 1981, Leslie and I began seriously freaking out. Something was very wrong. Too many bizarre things were happening. Dellentash flying off into the blue, money seeming to disappear, and the stories getting more and more unbelievable. What a mess.

Elizabeth Joel was Billy's manager, and she knew the ins and outs of the business. We went to see her and told her what we were afraid was going on. Leslie asked if *she* would manage us.

"Whoa! Whoa!" she said. "Not only can't I manage you, I can't have this conversation. I could get into big trouble. What I can do is give you the name of a very good lawyer. It is the only and best thing I can do for you right now."

The very first thing the lawyer asked was, "Where is the money?" and I said, "It's over in Citibank."

He said, "Do you have signature on it?"

I said, "Yes."

He got into the car with us and we all went to the bank. It turned out they didn't have my signature. Sonenberg and Dellentash or their accountant had given me the cards, had me sign them but never filed them. They'd apparently signed their own names to other cards and turned in those instead. The lawyers presented a letter to the bank telling them to freeze these accounts, but because I didn't have a signature on the account, there was nothing they could do about it. That simple act was the beginning of the downward spiral.

We had a meeting with Al Dellentash and told him we had serious misgivings about how he and Sonenberg were handling our affairs. We told him we wanted to change managers. His answer was not exactly what we'd expected.

"Well, you can do what you want but I'm going to have to tell you right now that if you leave, your career is over. And Meat? I really

love your kids, and I really *love* your wife and I think you are one of the hardest-working guys I have ever seen and I have a lot of respect for you, but there are people who have a lot invested in this situation and if you don't come back to us right now *you are going down.* Your career is over. You will never work again. Everything you have will be taken away from you including your name."

"You may be right," I said. "But I'll tell you what—you are going to know you have been in a fight."

At that point, we were given twenty-four hours or so to get our stuff out of Riverside Drive. My *Rocky Horror* jacket and boxes of family photographs were all in the basement. I never saw any of those things again.

It was obvious to me that in their eyes I was completely washed up, and not somebody they had to humor in any way whatsoever.

"Fuck him! He's over." That was their attitude. I was like an old hamburger wrapper; I was the disposable Styrofoam box.

It was like fighting city hall. They filed lawsuit after lawsuit. They were able to get court orders freezing every asset, every penny in every bank account.

Around the time of my meeting with Dellentash, I went to Marine Midland to take out some cash and found that all the money was frozen. Every cent. Even Leslie's little checking account, the one she used to write checks for groceries was frozen—it had four hundred dollars in it. There was one weekend that we had no money for milk for the children. In the end we had to borrow money from Leslie's parents to buy groceries.

Luckily I had ten thousand dollars in cash from a European tour that I kept in a safe, and once I got my hands on it that's how we survived. We'd moved out to Connecticut by then. The house was paid for—we'd paid for it outright. But because we didn't have a mortgage they eventually got that, too. Along with the cars, the furniture, the lawnmower. They even claimed in a lawsuit that they owned the name Meat Loaf. We got our lawyer to prove that I'd been called that in high school.

One day while we were away, the sheriff came in with a SWAT-like team to recover a Cadillac parked in our driveway. At the time we had a nineteen-and-a-half-year-old nanny looking after a one-

and-a-half-year-old baby and a five-year-old. She opened the door and the sheriff had a gun pointed at her head. The other guys were standing in the yard with assault rifles.

Out of the blue came outrageous stories about us in the press. It was as if someone had started a smear campaign. The stories said I was violent, that I had an arms cache in the house and had threatened people with guns, that I had slugged people in New Jersey. Not true. I haven't slugged anyone since I was in high school. Maybe a couple of plasterboard walls.

The rumors were relentless. Our lawyers said to just let it go, because if you respond with libel suits they just escalate and what's said about you becomes a fact. We couldn't afford it, anyway.

The slander got so bad that Leslie would go to the grocery store and they wouldn't take her checks. There was a drugstore where we'd had a charge account for years. The guy who owned it had read all the stuff in the papers and wouldn't let her charge. She put the items on the counter and he said, "What do I do? What do I do?"

"Let's see," said Leslie. "How about I give you the money and you give me the toothpaste?"

Creditors for heating-oil companies were harassing us. And it just got worse and worse. People were calling up Leslie and making up stories about me having orgies with groupies. A rumor even circulated that Leslie was having an affair with the chauffeur. *What* chauffeur?

It was unbelievable how ugly it got. You know how they never print someone's address in the paper? Well, they not only printed ours, they also managed to get a picture of my house and came close to including directions on how to get there! We had pickup trucks full of teenagers at two o'clock in the morning throwing beer cans at the house. Drunken teenagers yelling, "Wake up, scumbags." What can I tell you? I guess this is typical of fame in general. The harder they come, the harder they fall.

The lawsuits were like the paper circles of hell. They had sued me under every company that they had for breach of contract. The accounting company, the merchandising company, the touring company, the managing company. Every suit was five million dollars. I lost all those lawsuits. When Steinman sued me, that was the last straw.

We were advised to file for bankruptcy. Creditors came into

our home. They inventoried my pen, Leslie's watch, Pearl's Fisher-Price tape player. It was going to be one of those Willie Nelson lawn sales.

"Oh, you're gonna kill me?" I imagined myself saying to Sonenberg and Dellentash. "Well, fuck you anyway!" Just like the Monty Python bit in which the guy gets his arms cut off and then his legs cut off and then says, "Is that it?? Come back and fight me like a man."

To go through all of that and know there's nothing you can do about it. It was a living nightmare. From 1981 to 1991, it was ten years of pure hell. It was mind-boggling. Literally. Our minds were boggled, and stayed that way for years.

In 1983, the record company wanted me to do another album, *Midnight at the Lost and Found*. I had chosen huge piles of songs. They didn't want me to do any of them. "Okay, what songs am I to use?" I asked.

"You write them," they said. I ended up writing most of the songs on *Midnight*. One was called "Wolf at Your Door," which is pretty self-explanatory. I was only too familiar with that scenario by then. But I am not a great songwriter. The record company told me which songs to sing, how to sing them, what position to stand in, what musicians to use.

Even I wasn't happy with the stupid songs I'd written. I wasn't

happy with the way I was being treated. Eventually I turned to Tom Dowd, who was producing, and said, "Look, you finish it. I'm outta here." Unfortunately, this left them to do whatever they wanted to do and then put it out however they wanted.

But I couldn't deal with the record; I couldn't deal with anything. Leslie and I were both having nervous breakdowns. Simultaneously. I had already gone through one nervous breakdown and come out the other side of it. I had gone to a psychologist for a year about my voice (and the stupid business of being a rock star). The only reason we got up in the morning was the children.

When we lived in Stamford we had the IRS coming around wanting to dig up the basement and the backyard. Someone had told them that I had Krugerrands buried in the backyard. Hundreds of thousands of dollars worth of South African Krugerrands. I wish. When the IRS saw the way we lived, it wasn't hard to convince them that this was a figment of somebody's imagination.

The way I got through my days was playing softball. And coaching Little League. I played every day. It was like a major league schedule in softball. What I did in the winter, I have no idea. Wait for the softball season, I guess. I played with Belushi for a while. Al Pacino was on a team I played on later. All kinds of people roamed in and out of that game. In Westport I coached the girls softball team. When we moved to Stamford I coached Little League. I drafted the first girl ever into that Little League. She played second base. She couldn't hit for beans, but she could field. These kids are all thirty years old now. I saw one of them the other day. He said, "Do you remember me? I played first base for your team in Little League."

"You're kidding," I said. "You look thirty years old."

"I am," he said. "I'm thirty-two, actually."

Emotionally, how did I deal with it? I guess I didn't. It's like, how did I deal with my childhood emotionally? Blocked it out and went on. There is nothing I can do about what happened. I can tell you the story, but that's it—I can't change it. Well, there *is* one thing. I don't let management ever touch any money. I don't let any agency touch any money. I let only one guy touch the money, my friend Bernie Gilhuly. And if he takes it, well, *c'est la vie.*

bad attitude

On May 4, 1984, I went to England to record *Bad Attitude*, the album that I'd been working on with Paul Jacobs and his wife, Sarah Durkey. I lived in St. John's Wood, which was a block-and-a-half walk to Abbey Road Studios where we were recording.

I had talked to Jim about writing songs for the new album, but with Jim this is a process that goes on for years. And as usual, the record company wanted the album out yesterday. This time it was me who couldn't wait for Jim.

Alan Shacklock was the producer. He was fast and very organized but entirely wrong for me. His experience was in rock-and-roll and what I do is closer to musical theater. I choose my songs by the characters that are involved and how the scene breaks down. It's about becoming the character and then singing from that character's point of view. They are all scene studies really. Songs that aren't scenes never work for me. I did it for a while because we were trying to do what the record company wanted, what it thought would sell.

Bad Attitude was on its way to becoming a really good album—we'd been working on it since November of '83—there's "Modern Girl," on it and "Jumpin' the Gun," and "Piece of the Action." "Bad Attitude" was a great song. I did a duet with Roger Daltrey from the Who. He played the father, I play the son. We had an argument and that was the line he would say, "You have a bad attitude." We did it live. Daltrey is an actor himself, so he understood what I was doing. But we rushed it out and the album fell apart. I hadn't even learned my own lessons.

the death of wells kelly

I had Wells Kelly from the band Orleans playing drums for me on that album and Paul Jacobs on piano. The guitar player was Bob Kulick from back in '78. We used different musicians in and around London. Ellen Foley came over. Then drugs raised their ugly head again. Wells had had a problem with alcohol and   drugs. But we were currently on a health kick. Everybody had been running and exercising getting ready—we were two days from starting the tour. Wells had been clean, straight, and sober for a year or more. Every morning the guys would go jogging together. I'd stay in bed and protect the house. When I heard that everybody was going to a big party with the Huey Lewis guys I started to get nervous. I slept lightly. Later that night I heard Paul come back into the house. I asked him, "Is everybody back?"

He said, "No, we lost Wells."

An hour later I heard somebody come in the door and I thought, "It's him. Okay, everything is fine. Everyone is home." So I went to sleep. The next morning, it must have been nine-thirty, I heard somebody take off real fast through the wooden gate outside and right then I knew something was wrong. About five minutes later, I hear this commotion. I went downstairs and there was Wells on the front porch, bent over the wrought-iron railing. He was dead. It is a

very very sad story. Wells was apparently put in a taxi by these guys at the party—they knew there was something wrong with him. Wells managed to get himself home. He had overdosed on whatever but was still together enough to knock on the door. But because the girl who lived downstairs was a twelve-stepper in Alcoholics Anonymous, when Wells came back—and he was clearly drunk or high—she wouldn't let him

in. It was like, "Call me when you're sober," that type of thing. When they did the autopsy, they said that there wasn't enough of anything to kill him. Sometimes when somebody does a lot of drugs for years and years and then stops, even the smallest bit can kill them. Wells apparently thought he was doing cocaine and it was heroin. It was one of those "Oh come on, Wells. A little bit isn't going to kill you, man." And it didn't—right away. Scotland Yard called it "death by misadventure."

 # Arrest that movie

Eventually, the law got onto Dellentash's case. Along with his father, Al got busted in Baton Rouge. Something to do with distributing drugs. His dad, by the way, was a contractor for one of the floors of the World Trade Center. We read about it in the *Daily News*. I also read in the *Daily News* that I was going to be subpoenaed for the Gene Gotti trial (John Gotti's brother) and I was. I can only assume it had something to do with Dellentash, because he had turned state's evidence against a couple of people Gene Gotti was on trial with for heroin trafficking. Dellentash—who apparently copped some kind of plea in connection with his Baton Rouge arrest and was sentenced to five years in prison—testified during the Gotti trial that he had refused to get involved in smuggling heroin, but admitted he'd taken part in the marijuana smuggling operation.

I even heard he was in the witness protection program. The story has it that he had plastic surgery in order to change his identity and now looks like Richard Nixon on the skids.

One night, we were going to have the screening of the *Dead Ringer* movie for Robert Altman, because Alan Nichols had worked for him. When were all sitting in the screening room, Robert Altman was there and just as the credits started rolling, the lights go up and, since it was connected to the lawsuits with Sonenberg and Dellentash, in come the sheriffs and confiscate the film! Altman looked up and said, "That must be some hot movie!"

Your life sucks

I'm away on tour. Leslie's at home going a little crazy. She'd have a few drinks and call me up in the middle of the night and get nuts on the phone.

"I know there's someone there. Tell me who's in the room with you!"

"Honey, I'm here alone in room 809 watching *Star Trek* reruns." And I was.

Still, I couldn't blame her. All the pressure of bankruptcy, all the people feeding her stories about me. In the meantime, I was having my own kind of panic attack throughout most of '84 and '85, which probably didn't help. I'd watched everything that I had worked for disappear and I didn't want it to happen again. But to start that struggle back up the hill one more time was harder than doing it in the first place. Much.

I'm trying to get the *Bad Attitude* album off the ground, and in the meantime I'm fighting Cleveland International. I'm fighting CBS. I'm still fighting Sonenberg and Dellentash. And I'm still fighting Steinman's hatred of me.

All of a sudden in '85, I have the opportunity to pull out of the doldrums. I've got a record. I've got a tour up. But Leslie is still back there in the middle of the chaos. She's still living in that nightmare world of lawsuits and bankruptcy and harassment. I totally escaped it. I'm on the road in England.

Leslie and I had to be apart because we had no money, but during these separations we lost contact with each other. They were very destructive. While we were separated, Leslie started drinking heavily.

I had been gone on tour for five months and when I did get back to America, I didn't go home to Leslie. I rented an apartment in New York with this woman I'd met in Australia. I wouldn't tell her where I was, I wouldn't talk to her. I couldn't bring myself to tell Leslie I was planning to leave her. It only lasted a few weeks, but it was horrifying. Leslie was in the middle of a nervous breakdown and I ran away. Like I ran away when my mother got sick. I know I wouldn't do that today, after four years of this I was a crazy man myself. I'm ashamed to admit it, but when I started to get my career back I clung to it for dear life.

Leslie's much more emotional than I am. She dwells on things. She was desperate. She was in terrible shape mentally and physically. She weighed eighty-eight pounds.

First she went to see the minister of a church in Greenfield Hills, which is near Westport, for spiritual guidance, and he told her, "I really don't think that you would fit in with the community of this church."

Next she went to the Assembly of God, these fundamentalist Christians who speak in tongues and roll around on the floor, and they said, "Leslie, you have to get with the speaking in tongues thing because if you don't, it means that you have the evil spirit in you." When the tongues didn't speak through her, they said, "There is evil in you and that's why you are having these troubles in your life. The devil is in you and he is taking over your soul." She couldn't run out of there fast enough.

Finally she checked herself into Silver Hill in Connecticut, a rehab center for rich people. She drove herself there, but stayed for only five days. The doctor told her, "You are not ill and you're not an alcoholic. It's just that your life sucks. There's not really a whole lot we can do for you here. What you need is a good attorney."

The day Leslie threatened to start divorce proceedings, I woke up fast. I realized that I had put everything I loved at risk. I loved my family, I loved Leslie, I loved Pearl and Amanda—they were the most precious things in the world to me. I had lost everything else and I didn't want to lose that. I showed up the next day on her doorstep in tears. I told her I was sorry and that I loved her and that I loved our family and could I come home. And it was just, "Yes."

blind before i stop

Things were beginning to look brighter. I had a new manager and I'd finally found someone I could write with: John Parr. There was no point waiting for Steinman.

Work was going really well on the new album, *Blind Before I Stop*. John and I had just finished this duet called "Rock 'n' Roll Mercenaries." We were doing a sold-out show at Wembley Arena in London. John came on to do our duet. I never introduce people in the middle of a show—it breaks the continuity. I don't introduce the songs. You don't stop in the middle of a play and say, "And now, ladies and gentlemen, entering the stage is Robert De Niro." But John got so mad because I didn't introduce him that he walked off the stage, walked out of the building, and I have never heard from him since. No matter how many phone calls we made to him, he never called back. It destroyed our friendship. I tried like crazy to get in touch with him. I left messages apologizing. "John!! I'm sorry!! Please come home!!"

I had a new manager by now, Bob Ellis, who'd been married to Diana Ross. He suggested that I listen to one of the records Frank Ferian produced. They were great, there were amazing sounds on it. Frank is German and speaks almost no English at all, but he is a phenomenal producer. I've never worked with anybody who had an ear like Frank. He knew everything about what was going on inside a studio. He's famous for Milli Vanilli. The guy who actually sang on the Milli Vanilli cuts sang the background on the record I did with Frank Ferian. He had been doing this Milli Vanilli deal forever. I was one of the few people he ever produced who was the same person on the record and on stage.

Frank took these two Milli Vanilli guys from some club out of Saarbrücken. All they had to do was lip-synch and look good and they won a Grammy! This became something of a scandal when it came out, but what was weird was that Frank had done it for years.

I went to Frankfurt to work with Ferian and, at the end of June, I took home a mix of a rock-and-roll record. After I left, Ferian went back in and put a dance beat on every song, with the exception of one, a song called "Execution Day," which Dick Wagner had written. I had "Execution Day" as the last song on the album. Ferian changed the order of the album around and added all this dance-beat stuff. The first copy I got of the record was the promotional copy—it was already pressed. I remember putting it on the stereo in Westport and I'm thinking, "The order. They changed the order!" But before I call anyone I decide to just listen to everything.

First, I hear "Execution Day" and it's fine. The next song was "Blind Before I Stop" and I hear, underneath, dance-beat sounds. I think, "What the hell is that?" Then I listen to the next song and there's a dance beat underneath on it, too. And on *every* song.

"Oh my God, oh my God," was all I could say. I was sputtering. I call Bob Ellis. "I have got to stop this record. The order is wrong, the cover is wrong, and the *music* is wrong. They're trying to make me into Gloria Gaynor!"

"Meat, listen," he said. "Just do this record. This will be the last record you will have to do for Arista blah blah." Sure, Bob. And the check is in the mail.

I'm not an appliance

Arista Records had just been bought by General Electric. They literally took a guy from Minnesota who'd been in charge of appliances—a big shot, sure, but in the *appliance* division—and they brought him in to head the record company. I wanted him to promote the new single, but he wouldn't. The time had come to put my size ten-and-a-half foot down. I was supposed to go to this meeting with Bob Ellis, my manager at the time. Bob was a huge freak. The night before, he'd been out all night and was sleeping it off—not that Bob was exactly the voice of reason himself, he was given to punching people out who didn't see eye-to-eye with him. So I ended up going in there on my own to talk sense into this GE guy.

This was the conversation. I said, "You say you don't want to put out another single, but you're wrong about this. I think this is the perfect time to put out another single. The album is doing great. The last single took off. What are you waiting for?"

He said, "Well, Mister, uh, Meat Loaf? As you know, we *have* put out one single of yours." He was very pleased with himself.

And I said, "Yeah okay. You put out one and it did good. What did it get to here, ten?" I said, "That's pretty good, don't you think?"

He goes, "Yeah. That was good. But we think we've pretty much saturated the market with this cut from the album."

"People put out four and five singles from an album if it's a hit. You're only going to release *one?* You've got to put out another one, *now!*"

"NO!" he says. "I'm in charge here and we've looked at the accounting, we've looked at this—"

I said, "Have you heard the song?"

He said, "No."

I said, "Have you even heard the album?"

He went, "No, but I don't need to."

I said, "Well, how can you run a record company if you don't listen to the music?"

He goes, "Well, this is not about music. This is about what money we expend in the next fiscal—"

I said, "No, it is not. It's not about that. It's about the fucking music, you fucking moron!" He was stunned.

I just went crazy. I went completely loony. I lost it, and when I lose it, I'm *horrible*. I'm a horrible human being. I'm really bad. You ask my kids. You can ask my wife. You can ask anybody! I attack like a guard dog at Fort Knox. Go for the weakest things. Go for what I figure is the most vulnerable on anybody. Pin you on it and just go for the jugular. I attacked this guy. I lunged at him verbally like I was going to blister him with my rage. He was shaking.

"You stop it right now," he said. "No one has ever spoken to me like that before."

He was slumped back in his chair as if I had actually wounded him. He sat down and leaned forward and put his head on the desk. I thought he was going to burst into tears. But, guess what? Yep! They released the single!

I ran into Jim again at the end of 1985 at the Power Station in New York. I was in there mixing "Modern Girl." Steinman was there doing the second Bonnie Tyler album. I was in Studio B and he was in Studio A. We met in the hall and he said he had heard *Bad Attitude*, and he said to me, "It's not bad. It's pretty good."

I said, "Oh thanks."

He goes, "You're singing good."

I thanked him again.

He said, "Why don't you come out to the house?"

This was his house in Putnam Valley. He was living there by himself. He can't have anybody come in his space. It isn't selfishness on Jim's part, it's fear. I think he is terrified of contact. You can't even touch him. I am one of the only people who can even get near him. If I hug him, he accepts it. Occasionally, he will let Leslie give him a hug. Ordinarily, he won't let anyone touch him.

As soon as I got there we went out to the piano and started singing "Crying out Loud" and "Heaven Can Wait" and other things we both knew. Hanging out that day, he mentioned something about maybe we should think about doing a *Bat II*.

Jim and I wanted to start work on *Bat II* but Arista—incredibly!—didn't want it. Was the world not waiting for it? Weren't millions of fans clamoring for it? They said, with Steinman involved, it would cost too much. So, to fulfill our contract we made a live Meat Loaf album for

$17,000. Leslie's brother, Tommy Edmonds, mixed it, and that was that. The world would have to wait for great reawakening of *Bat*.

Al Teller, the president of CBS wanted the great new *Bat* opus but then he left and we would have to wait until 1988, when he went to MCA, for Batworks II to get under way.

Once again, I was forced to change managers. I liked Bob Ellis, but things had just become too crazy. Leslie and I went in the opposite direction this time. We chose George Gilbert and Walter Winneck as our new managers. They were very sensible people, and that's just what we needed.

the good guys

In 1987, the IRS audited me for the ten previous years, from 1977 until 1987. All this flying paper—five-million-dollar lawsuits and such—had caught their beady little eyes. One day this guy calls me, identifies himself as head of the Northeast IRS. I freaked. We have a car, a couch, a Sony television, a piano, and a dining room table. That is all we own.

He said to me, "Listen, I just want you to know, I am going to help you as much as I can. I have been working for the IRS for twenty-three years and I have seen a lot of things but yours is the worst case I've ever seen. We have had our agents down in the court-house looking through the court files. They've read every lawsuit, every paper, they've been through the bankruptcy with a fine-tooth comb. I have never seen anybody screwed over the way you have been. You are it!"

I believe it was this one man who pulled everybody off our backs. The IRS actually gave us a refund at one point. We've all heard those horror stories about the IRS, and that's all it would have taken to shove us right over the edge. But in this case they were the good guys. And then along came knighted business manager Bernie Gilhuly in 1989. He took this huge, massive ball of twine and unraveled it for us.

What is this, 1968?

When we finally got back on our feet emotionally, one of the first shows we did was in a place called Biddy Mulligans, in the suburbs of Chicago. We hadn't played in Chicago for ten years. We pulled up, and this place wasn't as big as a pool house. They'd fit the bands in by putting a big piece of plywood on these two long bars that went across the middle of the room. That's where the band played. On top of the plywood. We sat up on this piece of plywood and played the gig. There couldn't have been more than two hundred people in this place, but it was jammed. We had fun.

We put the amps down in the bar area and the drums on this plywood platform. The bartenders were ducking under the plywood getting all these drinks. It was wild. I remember the band saying, "Aw, c'mon, Meat, we can't do this."

I said, "Yeah, we can." I was used to dealing with anything by then.

In Las Vegas, we got to the club and they didn't have a PA. "Don't *you* guys have one?" they asked us.

"What is this, 1968? Who carries their own PA system anymore?" We had to put the vocals through a couple of Marshall amps.

There were the usual occupational hazards of rock on the road. The guitar player got so drunk one night that we thought he was dead. We waited like thirty minutes, then we started calling him and knocking on his door. We got a key and it was chained. Finally, the firemen came and took the door off. This was in Canada. He was still drunk when we got in there.

Another guitar player story. We were playing in Virginia Beach and in the middle of "Bat Out of Hell," I turn around, and I see the guy passed out on the piano. His guitar was just feeding back. I got so mad that I walked straight off the stage, up the aisle of the theater, and back to the hotel.

Then we had a bus driver from Alabama who couldn't read. We found this out the hard way. Not that there were any clues—we went into some really nice restaurants but it didn't matter, he would always order a cheeseburger and french fries. We were in Canada one morning at about six o'clock, and we'd been traveling all night. All of a sudden it got real quiet. The driver was coasting down a hill with the engine shut off. Pat Thrall went up front to the bus driver, and asked, "What are you doing?"

"Well, I've run out of gas. Shouldn't I go as far as I can?"

Pat said, "No!! Pull over now!" We'd run out of gas in the middle of nowhere. What was even more interesting was that we'd gone three hundred miles in the wrong direction, all because the guy couldn't read.

We were playing the tiniest clubs in all creation. But no matter what happened, I kept saying I couldn't cancel. One morning, our tour manager Matt Jett woke me up and said, "Meat, it isn't worth going to Alabama."

"No club too small," I mumbled from a dead sleep.

"Listen!" he said. "Here's the deal. The crew is there and they can't even get our equipment *into* the place." Turned out the club was an old 7-Eleven.

"Okay," I said. "Go back to sleep. I draw the line at 7-Elevens."

Mom-and-pop rock and roll

In the spring of 1989 our tour manager, Matt Jett, threw his back out to the point that he could not move. "But, listen," he said, "the tour coming up, it's a piece of cake. It's just the Stone Pony and a couple of clubs on the shore in New Jersey. It's all set up. You can do it yourself. Leslie could do it! It's like falling off a log."

Well, not exactly. He'd neglected to mention that one of these New Jersey club owners had threatened serious mayhem when Matt asked for the money. "How would you like me to break your kneecaps and take you for a boat ride?" Leslie was fearless though. She collected the money from this same guy, hopped on the bus, and said, "Step on it!" At another Jersey joint where they kept boa constrictors under glass, the promoter pointedly pared his nails with a bowie knife while discussing the band's payment.

Many places we played we didn't even take out newspaper ads. We would just put a sign in a store window: "Meat Loaf. 8:00 P.M. Tonight." It was hard for me at first. I'd come a long way, all right, but in the wrong direction. It was like being hit in the face with a big wet tuna.

We started out in small clubs that held four or five hundred people. Just small clubs and colleges. We would set up everything ourselves with a skeleton crew. Hey, we made a living. And we didn't have a record company to mess things up. It made life less complicated—and more fun. We just did it ourselves and had a good time.

Leslie just jumped right in and took over. She went to travel agent school. Once you are certified you can get 75 percent off your own ticket and 50 percent off your spouse's ticket. It is a TA discount. She would bargain. "Look. Don't even pay a commission. Just give me the cheapest rate possible for thirteen hotel rooms or give me the Meat Loaf Suite credit."

We had a basement office, a mom-and-pop rock-and-roll business. The kids would be upstairs doing their homework and we would be down there, making reservations and running all the budgets and creating the productions.

Between '87 and '92, we did it ourselves. Pearl and Amanda were going on tour with us by then. In the winter there wasn't that much work so we looked forward to spring and summer when we'd play the beach resorts.

In South Carolina we did a Chippendale Club. We went in there in the afternoon for sound check and you couldn't see a thing—the lights weren't good. Management's response was, "If they're good enough for the dancers, they're good enough for you." But lights were minor. The big argument centered around show time. They wanted me to go on at eleven at night. Past my bedtime. I like to go on at nine-thirty. They didn't want that because when I was done everybody would stop drinking beer and leave. If they got everybody in there at eight and I went on at eleven, they had three hours of beer, plus the beer while I was on, plus the people would be so drunk they'd stay till one in the morning. Of course, once they found out we were going to play for two and a half hours, they didn't mind as much!

We had Billy Sheldon designing lights and he is a genius. He would make the most beautiful lights. It was a great show. We had the two little blondes, Amy and Elaine Goff, who looked like twins, on tour with us. Blonde hair down below their waists. They wore these little leather miniskirts. Very sexy. But because Amy was so small and I'm so large, it was important to be careful that the seduction scene in "Paradise by the Dashboard Light" didn't look like a rape scene. We solved this by having Amy beating the crap out of me and triumphing at the end.

Sheik of araby

We toured in Germany and Scandinavia, England and Ireland, Italy and Spain, but the Middle East was something else. We played in Abu Dhabi, Oman and Bahrain.

As long as we entertained at the Hilton, and it was just Americans and English coming to the show, it was fine. But whenever any of the local Muslims would show up, the Boogie Police would appear. If an Arab started to dance, they would come over and tap him on the shoulder and tell him to stop.

We had to alter the women's costumes—arms and shoulders had to be covered—shoulders are considered as erotic as breasts in Arab countries. And absolutely no touching between men and women was allowed. This made performing "Paradise by the Dashboard Light" a little tricky. What we'd have to do was black out the stage during the making-out scene. In the darkness you would hear all kinds of lovemaking noises and then the lights would come back up for the marital argument scene.

After dinner one night, Leslie and I decided to go out for a walk. We went into the town to see what the nightlife was like. This consisted of enormous crowds of men on the street corners smoking, talking loudly, and gesticulating ferociously. You saw no women. Leslie was actually spat at, because women are not allowed out after dark and even if they are with their husbands. We almost got arrested holding hands and kissing on the street.

This seemed a little excessive, but for people who thirty or forty years earlier lived in tents like nomads, I just thought this must just be a residue of tribal morality. Now everybody was a petromillionaire and had two Mercedes in the garage.

There were some other customs, though, that were positively gothic. One day we saw a woman wearing a muzzle, albeit made from twenty-two-karat gold. It went across her mouth and wrapped around her neck. When Leslie saw this bizarre piece of jewelry, she asked our guide what it was. The guide went, "Shh!"

When we got into the car later, she said very matter-of-factly, "Oh, that was a wife's muzzle." I said, "A what?!" As if explaining some

meat loaf TO HELL AND BACK

quaint detail of Middle-Eastern life, she said, "Certain tribes, they have harems, yes? And the chief, he can be having as many as five wives. Custom used to be that husbands could muzzle wives if being pain in neck."

"But," I asked, "did this woman's husband actually put this contraption on her to keep her from speaking?"

"Well nowadays," she said, "sometimes older women who have husbands with younger wives are doing it to themselves. They have muzzles made and are putting them on to be showing they are subservient. Reason why they do this? Fear of being cast out on street and ending in ruin and devastation. They put you on street and you are having no home, and others are forbidden to let you in. You are doomed."

"Well, thank you for a lovely time," said Leslie. "But I really must be going."

larcenous priests and anarchy in the u.k.

In 1989, we also did nineteen towns in Ireland. We toured Ireland more than U2. There are not that many Irish bands other than the Irish folk bands that travel around. We were going to all these tiny little places and playing these shows where no one had ever made the effort to go before. It would take us forever on these tiny Irish roads in these really rickety old buses to get from one city to the next. You would have to stop the bus to let some little donkey cart pass by or let a flock of sheep cross the road. We stayed in a lot of old mansions where there were ghosts and things that go bump in the night.

Some of these places were so small that the local promoter might be a farmer or the pub owner. At one place, it was the parish priest. We set up the show in the parish hall of the town, and then we all had to eat dinner. While we're eating, we see the priest in his garb come around the corner carrying the ladder the carpenters had used to rig the show with. We stopped him and said, "Excuse me, sir. That's our ladder."

"Oh is it then?" he said. "And here I thought you wouldn't be needing it anymore now that you're done setting up. We could use a ladder like that at the church. We thought you might want to donate it."

Some of the venues were very basic. We pulled up to this one gig and there wasn't a house or another building in sight. Just a big barn in the middle of a field. I was looking around and saying to myself, "Okay. Who is going to come to this?" They were still empty-ing the hay out of the barn when we arrived. They had put a stage down at one end. I went inside and everybody was just standing around. I said, "Are we ready for sound check?"

They said, "Not quite. You see, the building has no power. And the thing of it is nobody thought about the barn having no power, this being the first time we've had a rock band here." Okay, no sound check. The doors open and people are coming in. By seven-thirty, there were easily three thousand people crammed into this building and we still had no power. Eventually, they had just enough power to run about three or four light bulbs on the ceiling. I know there were a few lights, because we could see the people. At eight o'clock the generator shows up and saves the day.

The audiences were very receptive to our shows, probably because our songs are all little dramas and the Irish love stories. They're great storytellers themselves, even in their songs. After the show, the whole band would sit there with their mouths open, mesmerized by this old guy telling stories of the Irish troubles over five hundred years in a song that seemed to go on for an hour and a half. No one was bored. We were all enraptured by this song that had been apparently handed down from generation to generation in this old bloke's family. It was like a prayer.

When we crossed the border from Ireland into Northern Ireland, we weren't aware how intense the feelings were between the Catholics and the Protestants. At one point Leslie got off the bus to walk around and when the promoter caught sight of her he was absolutely mortified. "Are you wanting to be shot?" he asked. "Do you understand what you're doing? You are wearing orange and it is such-and-such a day and this is a county that is completely Catholic and, well, that orange you're wearing is like a red flag to a bull." She had to go change her clothes. She was offending the whole town.

We had IRA members secretly on the bus with us in plain-clothes and we had the British Army in troop transports in front and behind our tour bus. The promoters had somehow worked out an agreement between the IRA and the British Army. They were working together to make sure no harm would come to us. We stayed at this hotel in Belfast called The Forum, and the place was completely surrounded by tank barriers and barbed wire. It was like being in Beirut. I remember driving from the radio station to another hotel, in County Antrim in the country. There were English Army troops everywhere in open lap bed trucks with guns at the ready. Leslie thought this would make an interesting photo, so she rolled down the window and started taking pictures. Once again, we almost caused an international incident. You can't take photographs of the Army.

In 1989, we were in Manchester on tour in England. We had just finished the gig, and after a show I like to do an Elvis, where I run off stage, put a towel around myself, and jump on the bus, soaking wet in my stage clothes. I'd done three in a row or something; I was exhausted and just wanted to go home and go to bed. We were on our way back to the hotel when the bus stopped at a stop light and I saw this guy beating up a girl on the street. I said, "Stop the bus! Stop the bus!! Open the door!" I ran out with this long towel around my shoulders, like a Superman cape, and went over to the guy and picked him up by his lapels and put him up against the wall and said, "Didn't your mother ever teach you not to hit girls?"

The guy looks at me and he goes, "Aren't you Meat Loaf?"

And I said, "Yeah! But that's not the point. The point is, you're not ever supposed to hit girls."

He says, "Jennifer, Jennifer, look! I'm being beat up by Meat Loaf."

"I don't care who the fuck you are," she says to me. "Mind your own fucking business!"

We did over two hundred shows a year. We were doing five nights a week, sometimes six, because our budget ran to twenty-five thousand or twenty-seven thousand dollars a week. If you are making five thousand dollars a show, you have to play six shows. It was hard, but it was also fun. I was singing really well and we were on the road constantly.

By the nineties, we got onto the festival circuit in Europe. Very good money. They would pay you seventy-five thousand to one hundred thousand, and we weren't even headlining then. The shows were great and there wasn't any pressure.

Things had turned around in the States for us, too. We'd left the clubs behind and were selling out the theaters. We sold ten thousand tickets at Ohio State. We had no record, no promotion, but *Bat Out of Hell* was going through the roof. On the first SoundScan chart, *Bat* was listed as the number thirty-six record in the U.S. Thirteen years after its release!

We were now doing over two hundred sold-out shows a year, and they were some of the best shows I have ever done in my whole life. I talked to Steinman and I said, "Jim, you have no idea what is going on out here. Come on the road for a week. It will blow your mind. It is the most amazing thing you can possibly imagine. *Bat* has risen from the grave and is flying high. We're back!"

bat 11

Getting together with Jim was easier said than done. He's the most infuriating person ever to make an appointment with. Whatever schedule you make with him, he'll cancel it. And it takes him forever to go anywhere. He's wracked by indecision. Jim can't even make up his mind about what he wants to eat. He'll order everything on the menu and every dessert *twice* rather than make a choice. He might take a bite out of each one and that's it.

Finally he shows up carrying his work in a couple of beat-up shopping bags from Bloomingdale's. I don't know how many leather carry bags I've bought him over the years, but the brown paper shopping bag seems to be his preferred briefcase. And soon as he pulls out a new song, you forgive him everything.

Christmas of 1990, Jim came out to our house in Connecticut to start working on the new album. Him at the piano, me pacing up and down—the same way we did the original *Bat Out of Hell*. He was late as usual, but when he played "I'd Do Anything for Love (But I Won't Do That)" for me, I melted.

The way Jim works on an album is this: First he recycles stuff that's either been lying around or, often, songs he's used elsewhere in another form. He re-records his songs with different people over the years until he finds the right place for it. His albums consist of little operas taken from a number of different years. A lot of songs on *Bat II* were ten years old or older. Some like "Good Girls Go To Heaven" had already been on Steinman solo albums. Steinman regurgitates the older material, then he writes three or four new songs, and that makes the album new. When he has the content down, then the album is ready to be recorded.

But it takes him forever. His tactic is delay. *Delay* delays and *negotiation* delays. For all his eccentricities, Jim is not simply the mad artist—he's extremely canny about business and strategies. He reads the trades, knows who's in, who's out, and who's head of programming. That's how he found out about Left Bank.

One day he said to me, "You know, Meat, most managers are cheerleaders. They hang out with the artist and pat him on the back but they can't call a radio station. They have no serious relationships with record company people or executives, hence they have a hard time affecting anybody's career."

"Was there something you wanted to talk to me about, Jim?"

"Meat, you really need to change managers. These guys you're using are completely inept. They can't handle it. I don't want to finish this record with these guys managing you. They're lame. The record company is just going to end up taking the album away from us. You've got to find somebody else."

Jim had read about this guy Allen Kovac in *Billboard*. He had a management company called Left Bank and had got Richard Marx money owed him by EMI.

Jim had given me only half the songs for the album and refused to give me any more until I got rid of my managers. I had two managers at the time, Walter Winneck and George Gilbert. They had served us very well between '86 and '91. We had made money, and they were honest guys. I liked them, and one the hardest things I've ever had to do was to fire them. But they would have been totally incapable of dealing with the record companies on *Bat II*—they were already losing control of it.

Jim and I went to see Kovac. I proceeded to tell him that we had always felt that CBS owed us money on *Bat Out of Hell*. I knew it was still doing phenomenally well and when SoundScan, the music industry tracking service, reported how actively it was selling, I was convinced. I told him, "There's a bunch of back royalties that we think are owed us." He looked at us and said, "I can get that for you. I can get that back." He made a settlement and we were happy with it.

Kovac came over to the studio and we played him the music for the new album. "You guys don't make records," he said. "You make events. And this isn't a record. You've got to make this album happen like an event."

But first we had to finish it. Jim had been ensconced in a mansion the record company had rented for him from Merv Griffin. He'd

been there for ages and still we had only five sides. Allen and his partner Jeff Sydney put Jim on a schedule. They told him, "Jim, if you can't finish this for the September deadline, we're going to have to bring in other writers and finish it ourselves."

We had one big fight over the mix of "Life Is a Lemon And I Want My Money Back." When I get mad, ten minutes later, I'm the sorriest human being ever on earth, and I regret every minute of it. I just want to say I'm sorry, give you a hug, give you a kiss. But, as Leslie reminds me, when you blow up like that, you have no idea the damage it can cause. People aren't waiting for your hug.

It was four o'clock in the morning, and I couldn't be held responsible for anything I say at that time. Because I'm not a person who's awake at four o'clock in the morning. Jim is. He smokes pot, listens to the mixes in these specially designed rooms. He's a really unique individual. He has a warehouse filled with amplifiers, a type Sony hasn't made for fifteen years. Jim loves the sound on these amps so he scooped up as many as he could find, along with a certain kind of small speaker. He's got them set up in these listening rooms. Jim gets a chair, his ashtray, sets up speakers on these plant stands, hangs drapes in special places around the room and it's an Adventure in Listening. I listen in my car, because a car is what I always judge everything by. If it's any good in a car, it's fine. When Jimmy listens to mixes, he dissects them, he enters the music, he picks *this* little guitar string and *that* little note. It will make you crazy.

It took a long time to get *Bat II* done. Jim's songs may be miniature operas, but they're always too long for radio. Practically every one of them has to be edited down from nine or eleven minutes to something that the stations will play. He goes through incredible agony over these edits. As far as he is concerned, it'll *kill* the song.

He calls them his autistic children. He thinks of his songs as his babies, and when people start chopping bits of them out he goes through torture. He'll get on the phone and plead their case in the most heart-wrenching way, trying to get me or Leslie to champion his cause, to go to management or the record company or whomever the powers may be, and explain to them why the song can't be edited.

"I'd Do Anything for Love (But I Won't Do That)" started out fifteen minutes long. Allen Kovac was telling him, "You gotta cut nine minutes, Jim. This is never gonna get played on radio."

Jim was inconsolable, crying in front of everybody. "It's my baby, you're butchering my baby!"

He got in a huge fight with Allen over the edit of "Anything for Love." They were still fighting about it when "Anything for Love" had been number one for five weeks. Allen warned Jim that any song longer than five minutes wouldn't get air time on the radio. Jim is saying, "Well, it's five twenty-three, that's almost the same thing"

"Do you or do you not want your song played on the radio?" Allen asks him.

Jim digs in and says, "Oh, twenty-three seconds shouldn't make any difference." Allen agrees that it shouldn't, but it does! Jimmy's answer to any objection about length is, "What about 'Bohemian Rhapsody'?" It's a lengthy semiclassical piece that's a famous exception to the rule. The clincher in these disputes is always, "If we don't make the cut, the record company will, and the last thing anybody wants to see is a record company edit." Jimmy went along with it and then even after we cut it down he sent his own versions to the radio stations. That was six years ago, and Jimmy still hasn't gotten over it.

"I'd Do Anything for Love (But I Won't Do That)" wasn't hard to sing, but it was a bit of a problem getting it *right*. You really have to keep that thread taut all the way up until the girl comes in, because it's not a standard duet. It's got to be real tense for the surprise to work. When you're dealing with a song that's seven minutes long you can never lose focus.

The girl's part doesn't come in for six minutes. And clearly it can be confusing, because almost everybody comes up to me and says, "C'mon, Meat, what is *that*?"

I always think, "Ah, *man*!" Jimmy saw it coming. He said to me at the time, "Do ya think they're gonna get what *that* is?"

I'm saying, "Jimmy. How can they *not* get it? It's right there in the song, it's the first line before every chorus, like: 'I'll never stop dreamin' of you every night of my life. I'll do anything for her, but I won't do that.' How can they miss it?" They missed it. Plain as day.

Jimmy always said, "You know what? Nobody's gonna get it." And he was right.

ḣappy bob

The feeling between Jim and me was so positive after *Bat II* came out that Jim actually came and played in the show. It was pretty wacky. Jim likes to play the comedian, and one-on-one he's a very funny guy, but as a performer, sometimes his timing can be a little off.

Everybody got behind the *Bat II* tour. I'd never had this kind of support from the industry before. Even the review of the album in *Rolling Stone* wasn't the usual massacre. But when they reviewed the concert in Madison Square Garden and gave us a rave—four out of five stars—I almost had a heart attack and died. I literally got dizzy, almost fainted. Tripped over the couch.

We did 215 shows for the *Bat II* tour. I had the inimitable Patti Russo opposite me. Patti is a great actress, singer, and comic. She is willing to go way out on a limb. And she has infallible timing.

We got the girls in the show dressed up in different costumes. Cheerleader costumes. Or waitresses. This year it was a wedding. A couple of years ago, she was a dominatrix. She came out with a bull whip. We try something different for every tour.

Happy Bob came into our concert life with the *Bat II* tour. I redesigned the set, had new props and backdrops made, but there was still something missing. I wanted something really dramatic. Then the idea came to me while I was watching *This Is Spinal Tap.* "We should get ourselves a big inflatable bat," I said. Quickly adding, "That's thirty feet, not inches."

We came up with a design for a giant bat with glowing yellow eyes and a twenty-five-foot wingspan but we bought it without seeing it inflated. The bat made its first appearance in Zurich. As we're playing "Bat," up flies this giant inflatable critter. You couldn't exactly call it a bat. It looked more like a big yellow, grinning chicken. That's how it got the name, Happy Bob. People went crazy when he came lumbering up. They started applauding, but they didn't exactly know what they were looking at. "What the hell is that?" they were asking themselves.

Everybody in the band was cracking up and I was laughing so hard I could barely sing the song. We hired an artist to make him look more frightening. This was in '94. This year, we painted him again in Birmingham, because he was getting a little raggedy. He got even darker and more menacing, but he was still slightly goofy. Happy Bob is retired now. My inflatable period is over.

í vanished into thin air

After *Bat II* came out I went back to Dallas. We played Moody Auditorium at Southern Methodist University. Over the years lots of stories had gotten back to me about people I'd known in high school. One guy was involved in the savings and loan stuff and got sent off to golf jail. Some guys were divorced, this one wound up with that one, another one's a bum, some are alcoholics (pretty much all of them), and "wouldja believe so-and-so got thrown out of a Mexican restaurant for having sex with some guy in a booth?" Oh man, high school was never like this.

And all these people I'd known so long ago came to see the show. It was something strange, I'll tell you. I'd fled Texas twenty-five years earlier, but most of my friends had stayed down there in Dallas since high school. It's a whole other world, and it was suddenly looking incredibly odd to me, as if I were looking into the past through the bottom of an empty Lone Star bottle.

All of a sudden here comes Raymond Puckett talking in that Dallas drawl. He's "Hiya, man, h'ar ya?" I remembered Raymond's sister well. She was gorgeous! A cheerleader for the University of Texas. And Raymond was this really good-looking guy who played college football; he played end.

It was getting a bit weird. All these guys I'd known. They're fat, they've got bad teeth, balding, talking in that hokey way, telling me these stories about when I was a kid. Just a really *odd*-looking bunch. Leslie's with me, and she's whispering in my ear, "Who *are* these people?" Like maybe I had some deep dark secret in my past I hadn't told her about.

I was just starting to wonder if Billy Slocum was going to come, and then there he was. A little heavier; black, curly hair—it's graying now—but basically he looks exactly like he's supposed to look in my head. He was there by himself. He'd been standing in the back and he came down front. He was nervous to see me, I could feel it. We were standing in the aisle of this auditorium, awkwardly shifting our weight from foot to foot the way you do when you see friends you haven't seen in a long time.

meat loaf TO HELL AND BACK

"Billy," I said, "how *are* you? It must be, what? Fifteen years?"

He just stared at me and said, "I can't believe it's you."

I said, "What are you talking about? I'm the guy who was riding shotgun with you when you drove your truck through that plate glass window."

He says, "Nah, you're Meat Loaf—*the legend!* I cannot believe it."

"Aw," I said, "Billy, you know me. I'm just the plumber, man." And I gave him a hug.

It was so bizarre to me because Billy Slocum in high school was the king of the world. I wanted to *be* Billy Slocum. He was voted most popular and best-looking. He went out with the most popular girl: Donna White. She was a cheerleader and they eventually got married—and divorced. Billy raced motorcycles in the AMA—a bona fide motorcycle racer. Played football at San Houston State College. His family was wealthy—they owned a big printing company. They had the Frito Lay account! And he was friends with Ward Lay—in Texas that's a big deal.

There'd always been a sophistication about Billy and it was still there—he was still Billy as far as I was concerned. But for him, Meat Loaf, the guy who used to fix motorcycles with him, was gone. I was no longer there. In his mind I'd just vanished.

lose the palm trees

After making *Bat II* I felt I really needed to get back to acting. They were no longer casting that many movies in New York, so that meant moving to LA. Bernie Gilhuly started the wagon train—he was the first to move out to the West Coast. I was all for it. I didn't want to deal with the cold weather anymore, and I didn't want to go back to Texas, so LA was the logical choice. But Leslie resisted the move to California tooth and nail. She thinks everybody out here is crazy. Something to do with it being a desert and all those palm trees. She won't live in a house with palm trees in the yard.

Softball had always been the grounding element in my life, but in LA it became golf. And golf led to the movies. It all started with my friend and partner (and fellow Texan) Brett Cullen. I joined a golf club. There were a bunch of actors as members: Joe Pesci, Sean Connery, and Bill Murray. I even got up the courage to say to Joe Pesci one afternoon while he was putting, "Hit the fucking ball, you fucking whacko!" Hey, this acting thing was going to be fun.

One day, Brett and I were playing golf with a director named Peter Chelsen. He ended up giving me a part in a movie called *The Mighty*. Another of Brett's golf pals, Dennis Quaid, put me in *Everything That Rises*. Then the dominoes started to fall. Since then I've been in *Black Dog, Outside Arizona, Crazy in Alabama, The Fight Club, The Ballad of Lucy Whipple*, and *Rustin*, a little independent feature in which I finally get to play a football coach and use all those things football coaches ever screamed at me, like: "You look like Tarzan, but you play like Jane." Well, actually, nobody ever said I looked like Tarzan, but...you get the picture.

Escape from hell

Bat II had been so successful that soon—a couple of years, we're talking the Steinman time scale after all—there was talk of a *Bat III*. There were optimistic meetings with Jim. Two-thousand-dollar dinners at which Jim orders everything on the menu. Jim was throwing out tempting song titles like "God Has Left the Building." We said, "Wow!" Although I should have known better, we all started to believe he might actually have a whole album in embryo, tucked away in one of his ratty old shopping bags. His method is seduction. Jim has ideas for new stuff; he doesn't always have the songs. He was romancing us, talking himself into all these visions. If he can talk you into it, he can do it—eventually.

Bat III ended up becoming *Welcome to the Neighborhood*. It's a story album. Basically a guy's life story from the time he went on his first date to the present. I used pulp-fiction artwork for the cover and the booklet, with the lurid paintings and titles from forties detective magazines.

Allen had originally wanted to call *Welcome to the Neighborhood*, *Escape From Hell*, to link me to my own heritage. I wanted to do a Meat Loaf record, not more of Steinman's characters. I was screaming at Allen and saying, "I'm sick and tired of being a cartoon, I don't want to be that Meat Loaf comic book character any more."

When it was all over, I thought about what Allen had said. He looks at me and says, "You *are* a cartoon character. Look at your videos. Look at what you do on stage. That's what people love about you, you're larger than life."

So, instead of rejecting the cartoon, I would embrace him. I was going to bring that cartoon to life, put him in living color and take him on the road. And that's what I did. I came to the realization that, like Popeye, "I yam what I yam, and that's all that I yam": Meat Loaf, Meat Loaf Aday, Michael Lee Aday, Poor Fat Marvin, M. L. Aday, Meaty (to Sarah Ferguson), Sex God, Bubby (Leslie's Husband), and Dad, Pearl and Amanda's father.

acknowledgments

We would like to thank those who generously contributed to this book: Mary Alice Hukel, Virginia Elizabeth Allen Edmonds, Cecil Boyd, Sam Ellis, to Jimmy for writing such beautiful songs, Brett Cullen, Bernie Gilhuly, Allen Kovac and Jeff Sydney, Earl Shuman, Jordan Berliant and Carol Sloat (for their sleepless nights), Gary Stiffelman, Miles Levy, Karla Devito, Rory Dodd, J.J. Aronson, Ed Thomas, Robin Baum, John Sykes, Gay Rosenthal, Janet Alhante, Catherine Furness, Judith Regan, Lauren Field, Paul Olsewski, Andre Becker, Al Teller, Paul Conroy, John Giddings, Jonny Podell, Jonathan Levine, Curt Chaplan, and Patricia, Pearl, Amanda, Leslie, Winnie, and Gussie.

We would also like to thank Diane Le Page, Bob Quandt, Mary C. Pause, Sharon Ruetnick, Jonah Shaw, Claudia Gabel, Cassie Jones, Patricia Wolf, Dan Cuddy, Robin Arzt, Susan Kosko, Paul Brown, Jim Freek, Alan Fitzpatrick, Sneuques, and Toby Dalton.

Last but certainly not least, we owe a debt of inexpressible gratitude to our intrepid editors, Coco Pekelis and Jeremie Ruby-Strauss, without whom this book would not be.

photo credits

contents

part 1

part 2

part 3

Page 194-195:Leslie Aday
Page 199:   Ken Regan/Camera 5, Inc.
Page 200:   Epic Records
Page 205:   Leslie Aday
Page 211:   Bill King

part 4

Page 217:   Timothy White
Page 218:   Leslie Aday
Page 220-221:Chris Minerva
Page 225:   Chuck Pulin/Star File
Page 231:   Phyllis Hand
Page 241:   Mick Rock/Star File
Page 246:   Leslie Aday
Page 248:   Arista Records
Page 251:   Walt Disney Productions, 1979 (bottom)
Page 254:   Leslie Aday
Page 256:   Leslie Aday
Page 258:   Neal Preston
Page 263:   Arista Records
Page 267:   Neal Preston
Page 273-274:Neal Preston
Page 279:   PG Brunelli
Page 281:   Timothy White
Page 282:   Neal Preston
Page 283:   Neal Preston
Page 286:   Steve Rapport

color insert

1: 20th Century Fox
2: Ken Regan
5: TNT
7: Tri-Star Pictures
8: Neal Preston
9: Greg Allen
10: Neal Preston
11: Neal Preston
13: Matt Stone and Trey Parker
16: Steve Rapport

All other photos courtesy of the author's collection.